Expert Systems for Scanner Data Environments

International Series in Quantitative Marketing

Editor:
Jehoshua Eliashberg
The Wharton School
University of Pennsylvania
Philadelphia, Pennsylvania, U.S.A.

Previously published books in the series:

L. Cooper and M. Nakanishi: Market Share Analysis
D. Hanssens, L. Parsons, and R. Schultz: Market Response Models:
Econometric and Time Series Analysis

Expert Systems for Scanner Data Environments
The Marketing Workbench Laboratory Experience

John M. McCann
John P. Gallagher
The Fuqua School of Business
Duke University

Kluwer Academic Publishers
Boston/Dordrecht/London

Distributors

for North America: Kluwer Academic Publishers
101 Philip Drive, Assinippi Park, Norwell, MA 02061 U.S.A.

for all other countries: Kluwer Academic Publishers Group,
Distribution Centre, Post Office Box 322, 3300 AH Dordrecht, The
Netherlands

Library of Congress Cataloging-in-Publication Data

McCann, John M.
    Expert systems for scanner data environments: the marketing
workbench laboratory experience / John M. McCann, John P. Gallagher ;
with Bill Lahti ... [et al.].
        p.   cm. — (International series in quantitative marketing)
    Includes bibliographical references and index.
    ISBN 0-7923-9076-8
    1. Marketing—Data processing.   2. Consumer goods—Marketing—Data
processing.   3. Expert systems (Computer science)   4. Optical
scanners.   I. Gallagher, John P.   II. Lahti, Bill.   III. Title.
IV. Series.
HF5415.125.M4   1990
658.8′00285′642—dc20   90-38154
                                                                           CIP

CONTENTS

LIST OF FIGURES

PREFACE

This book is about the role of expert systems in marketing, particularly in the consumer goods industry. Section I describes the changing nature of consumer marketing and presents the rationale and need for expert systems. The remainder of the book combines a tutorial on expert systems with a series of expert system prototypes.

The tutorial material is presented in three places. First, section II is devoted to introducing expert systems in general. Chapter 3 provides a general introduction to the topic, which is continued in chapter 4 where a small expert system (the Promotion Advisor) is used to illustrate the important features of a backward-chaining, rule-based system. The promotion theme is extended in chapter 5 where a larger system is presented. The material in all three of these chapters was designed as an introduction and tutorial on the most common technology for building applied expert systems: the backward-chaining, rule-based inference engine.

Tutorial material is also contained in the body of the chapters that describe the prototypes. This material is usually in the form of sample rules and a description of the process for applying the rules. The third location of the expert system material is in chapters that follow discussions of the prototypes. Chapter 7 is a technical chapter on the coupling of expert systems to traditional systems. Chapter 11 describes model-based reasoning and its application to DEALMAKER, which is presented in chapter 10. This material introduces frame-based systems, which go beyond the backward-chaining, rule-based inference systems. Chapter 12 describes additional research in the application of expert systems to marketing problems. Chapter 13 discusses the implementation of marketing expert systems in a number of different firms.

ACKNOWLEDGMENTS

This book is based upon research conducted during 1986 and 1987 in the Marketing Workbench Laboratory at Duke University's Fuqua School of Business. We would like to thank Dean Thomas Keller and Associate Dean Richard Staelin for their support in the establishment of a somewhat non-traditional research center. The laboratory had major support from the IBM Corporation, and its creation and continued success was greatly enhanced by the strong support of Erich Baumgartner and Robert Bodie of IBM's Process Industry sector. The laboratory has benefited tremendously from the financial backing and encouragement of a large number of firms, including Pillsbury, General Foods, R. J. Reynolds Tobacco, Campbell Soup, Procter & Gamble, Carnation, Sara Lee, Colgate-Palmolive, Kraft, General Mills, Quaker Oats, Beechum, Bristol Myers, Ogilvy & Mather, Coca-Cola, Ocean Spray Cranberries, Nabisco, A. C. Nielsen, SAMI/Burke, James River, Frito-Lay, Clorox, Johnson & Johnson, and Sterling Drug. The authors' ideas and computer applications were derived from meetings and discussions with hundreds of managers in these firms.

The senior authors, John McCann and John Gallagher, would like to acknowledge the important role played by the book's supporting authors, who were responsible for writing the knowledge-based systems discussed in this book. Paula Ecklund authored the Baby Promotion Advisor discussed in chapter 4, and the expert system portion of the Marketmetrics Knowledge System discussed in chapters 6 and 7. Ali Tadlaoui researched and authored the Textbook Promotion Advisor presented in chapter 5, and the Promotion Detective system described in chapter 9. Kevin Walker programmed the Model Animation System discussed in chapter 8. Justin Hill wrote the SAS portion of the Marketmetrics Knowledge System as well as most of the operating system commands which allowed the knowledge system to interact with SAS. Bill Lahti designed and developed DEALMAKER, with the support of Justin Hill, which is described in chapters 10 and 11. All of these authors participated in the writing of this manuscript.

We would like to express a special thanks to Michelle Burnett for her untiring work and good cheer in administering the laboratory's many functions, and in her efforts to bring this manuscript to fruition.

Expert Systems for Scanner Data Environments

SECTION I:

THE CHANGING MARKETING WORLD

CHAPTER 1

THE MARKETING DATA EXPLOSION: THE PROMISE AND THE REALITY

> *It is now technically possible to wire up the nation so that a corporate marketing executive can get instant reports on sales as they happen. And that leads to a fantasy view of the future brand manager, sitting like Captain Kirk on the bridge of the starship Enterprise, getting reports on sales and then directing the specialists in his marketing crew to pour on instant consumer incentives where competition demands.[1]*

INTRODUCTION

Changes create opportunities. Today, changes in the amount and quality of available data are creating opportunities in the world of consumer packaged goods marketing. The older store audit and warehouse withdrawal data is being replaced by new scanner data and data associated with the scanner data. The resulting integrated, single-source databases promise to change the way consumer goods firms do business.

These data present an opportunity to improve the performance of marketing management by bringing information to bear on marketing decisions. In addition, the development of new models of brand performance enhances the impact of these new data. New computer systems make it possible for marketing managers to manage and understand the information the data and models contain.

But, there are a number of barriers that must be overcome before these opportunities can be realized. These barriers involve a mismatch between 1) the magnitude of the data and its implications and 2) the number of knowledgeable and experienced people required to capture the opportunities.

The new data has arrived at a time when research in artificial intelligence is producing technologies that allow for the development of computer systems that contain the knowledge of marketing experts. This chapter describes this new data, its sources, the technologies that explain it, the opportunities it presents, and the barriers to realizing those opportunities. Subsequent chapters will discuss how expert systems can deal with those barriers and help realize those opportunities.

DATA SOURCES

Data Collectors

The microprocessor is bringing about a major revolution in the data available for market research. Microprocessors, the "computers on a chip", are the key elements in this revolution. As computers become smaller and cheaper, they allow innovative developers to create an increasing array of instruments for collecting marketing research information.

The UPC scanner is the core element in this community of data collection instruments. The UPC scanner in a supermarket stores data about the prices and movements of every item in the store as part of the normal operation of the store. No special effort is required to collect these data. In a sense, the data are like apples growing on a tree that was planted to provide shade; they are a side product that require no additional effort or expense to collect.

The UPC scanners are popular because, among other things, they are becoming cheaper due to the declining price of microprocessors. These declining prices are also making possible other forms of measuring instruments:

- Hand-held computers with an attached UPC wand for use in collecting data about displays within the stores.

- Computers that "watch" television for the purpose of detecting and classifying commercials by what commercial was aired on what station in what market at what time. They are people meters for recording which individual in which household is watching which television station at what time. Some of these meters are equipped with equipment that lets the meter know when someone has entered or left a room. An infrared lens, located on top of each television set, scans the room and passively monitors how many viewers are present.[2]

- Household scanner instruments for recording the UPC code of purchased items.

- Smart cards for recording and storing customer purchase information at the store checkout counter.

These developments have an impact on three databases: store data, scanner panel data, and scanner census data.

Scanner Data

Retailers sell store level scanner data containing the price and movement of every UPC item to data vendors, research companies, and manufacturers. The data vendors augment these data by monitoring store display activity, retail newspaper advertising, and coupon distribution. Data are also available on the television advertising gross rating points that can be integrated into these data. The result is a weekly database that can be purchased at several levels of aggregation: market, chain, and store.

Scanner Panel

The data vendors also operate scanner panels in a number of markets that provide additional data on household purchase dynamics. An examination of one of these databases, the Nielsen SCANTRACK household panel, reveals the extent of the data at the household level:

Products purchased
  store shopped
  retail price paid
  coupons used

Promotion exposure
  in store: displays and retailer ads
  in home: coupons and promotion offers

Television viewing by households and persons
  commercials
  programs

Print advertising
  magazines
  newspapers

Household characteristics

Scanner Census Data

A number of technology developments may lead to a database that is more of a census than a small sample like the scanner panels.

In late 1986 Ukrop' s, a small retail chain in Richmond, Virginia, tested a barcoded ID card for distributing and cashing in coupons.[3] Most of the chain' s customers were issued cards provided by Citicorp POS Information Services.

Upon enrolling, the consumer was given a personal account into which coupons are electronically deposited. Each month the consumer receives a statement showing the coupons that have been deposited into the account. When the consumer shops, he or she is identified by passing the card through a slot scanner. As his or her groceries are scanned, the system automatically credits the consumer with any coupons that are stored in the system for items passing over the scanner. All of the data are sent to Citicorp, along with the identification of the shopper. Similar programs are underway at several different vendors.[4] The result is a sort of a scanner panel " census" that includes almost all of the chain' s shoppers.

In addition, supermarkets are using electronic-payment networks that allow their customers to use bank automated teller machine cards instead of cash to pay for groceries.[5] The result is the linking of consumer purchases with household identification. Systems could contain only the dollar amount of the purchase, or they could be developed to capture the detailed data at the UPC item level.

These two services, the smart card for promotion distribution and the electronic payment network, could be combined to produce a nationwide network in which every purchase of most of the population is captured at the point of purchase.

Mergers of Data Vendors

The research firms that offer these different types of scanner data are merging and beginning to offer databases that integrate the different data sources. The goal of these mergers seems obvious: a single-source supplier of data for use by marketing and sales managers. In 1984, the syndicated data industry was characterized by multiple data vendors (with each vendor having a piece of the total data needs). These vendors included Dunn & Bradstreet, A.C. Nielsen, IRI, Burke Marketing, SAMI, TRIM, Majers, Arbitron, BAR, and NPD. By 1988, there were three: Dunn & Bradstreet (with Nielsen, Majers, TRIM, and NPD), Control Data (with Burke, Arbitron, SAMI, and BAR), and IRI.

The new databases from these vendors are often referred to as " integrated" because they provide data from *all* sources. These data contain both outcome results and causal factors. Such integration permits marketing firms to develop models that relate results with their causes.

SUPPORTING TRENDS

Market Models

As data collectors have made more data available, marketing researchers have created models to interpret it. During the 1980s marketing managers have come to accept models of new product and promotion success. Models such as BASES, ASSESSOR, and PROMOTER have been validated and accepted by management, creating a positive climate for marketmetric models.

But, where the old data and models were able to show what happened, the new data and models show why it happened. These new models do not just show what volume has been, they quantify the relationship between a brand item's volume and the factors that influence that volume, the causal factors. Marketing researchers recognize the importance of this change. Len Lodish concluded in his 1986 book that status reporting has had little impact on profits.[6] But, he argued that market response reporting has and will lead to higher profits.

Researchers have already created many response models that use the scanner data. Work by Blattberg & Wisniewski[7] and Wittink, Addona, Hawkes, & Porter[8] have shown that it is possible to develop informative models of brand items using scanner and associated data. Guadagni and Little[9] have made similar advances with scanner-panel data. McAlister[10] has illustrated the types of insights that managers can obtain from such models. Blattberg and Levin[11] have developed models for measuring the effectiveness and profitability of trade promotions. Klein[12] illustrates a model for measuring the effectiveness of coupon promotions. Marketing management information systems such as EXPRESS or ANALECT contain the statistical procedures that make it possible to create these types of models.

Computer Systems

There are several developments in computer systems which enable managers to better take advantage of the new data:

Data management. The newer relational database systems such as SQL are making it possible to manage the masses of data as well as quickly extract the data necessary for any one model. In addition, modeling systems such as SAS are being extended to offer interfaces to these database systems.

Connectivity. Technology is advancing rapidly for connecting workstations to mainframes. This connection allows the system to distribute the computing to the machine which makes the most economical sense.

Workstations. The new workstations based upon 32 bit microprocessors are making it possible to develop model management and animation systems that can be distributed to the managers' desks.

Graphics. The graphics capabilities of these new machines allow managers to see and to understand what these models mean. Using graphics to make models easier to grasp is called *model animation*.

Computer literacy. The people moving into the brand groups are more computer literate every year, resulting in brand groups that are more interested in using advanced computer applications.

Local Focus Marketing

With finer-grain nature of the data, a manager can understand and develop marketing programs for smaller markets than was possible before. This ability is leading to the notion of local focus marketing, or marketing aimed at smaller and smaller markets.

Alvin Toffler was one of the first to foresee this focus:

The mass market has split into an ever-multiplying, ever changing set of mini-markets that demand a set of continually expanding range of options, models, types, sizes, colors, and customization.[13]

Similar comments were made by marketing managers in the firms who participated in the study that led to **The Marketing Workbench**[14]:

It used to be if you mentioned regional, the response was "too inefficient, we are a national brand." Now, emphasis on regional is much greater.

The world is very different from the way we have defined it in the past; we need to develop spending principles which recognize regional differences.

The concept of a national brand is becoming a figment of our imagination.

For this company to achieve its objectives, it must go to local focus and learn how to better manage marketing data.

We "big-pictured" it because we were limited to national numbers in static report form; we need to view "little pictures" in 60 markets.

We will bite the bullet and do everything regionally.

We built a "mega-database" in Lotus 1-2-3 which contained a lot of data from many sources. We did this because we were frustrated with not being able to understand local markets.

Regional marketing has become so important that we have put ten zone marketing managers in the field; they analyze local markets and prepare regional marketing programs.

Concrete moves have been made by several leading firms to implement local focus. Campbell Soup put in place 88 regional marketing managers as a means of implementing local marketing. In addition, the company considered the idea of splitting itself into four regional companies.[15] Frito-Lay[16] went to regional marketing via a zone marketing manager concept in order to combat local competition. Procter & Gamble[17] was reported to be considering alternative organizational structures to deal with local marketing. And, General Foods[18] tested a regional marketing approach in the Denver market.

Coupled with new response models and increasingly accessible computers, local focus marketing provides an opportunity to gain a significant competitive advantage in the marketplace. These advances promise to allow a brand group to give the same kind of attention to a store-level market that they currently give to much larger markets. Finally, a national brand group can compete at the same focused level that local brands use, while retaining the advantages of a national brand.

BARRIERS

But, brand groups, as they are structured today, cannot capture these opportunities. The magnitude of the tasks would overwhelm them. There is simply too much to do: too much data, too many markets, too few resources.

Too Much Data

Marketing databases contain information on the following dimensions: measures on items in markets over time. The number of measures, items, markets, and time periods determine the size of the resulting databases. The new databases are much larger than the Nielsen or SAMI based databases. To illustrate the difference in magnitude, the size of a database containing three years of data for a product category which is made up of 1000 items, has been calculated for Nielsen data, SAMI data and scanner data. The scanner data is broken into market, chain, and store levels. One thousand items is not a large category; the Italian sauces category contains over 2000 items.

Nielsen Store Audit Data. Nielsen store audit data were collected on a bi-monthly basis in about 20 markets. Due to the lengthy nature of the audit process, the data did not contain information on all of the items in the category. Assuming that only 20% of the items were monitored, and that 20 measures (unit sales, dollar sales, display space, etc.) were taken. The resulting database would contain 1 million numbers. This database would be updated with new data every ninth week, producing about 50,000 new numbers that the brand group would have to analyze.

SAMI Warehouse Withdrawal Data. SAMI data were collected on a 4-week basis, and contained about 20 measures. Assuming that 50% of the items were monitored, the result is a database containing about 20 million numbers. About 0.5 million new numbers would arrive every fourth week.

Market Level Scanner Data. Scanner data are collected weekly and all the items in the category are monitored. Assuming that 30 measures are taken in 60 markets, the result is a database of about 280 million numbers. About two million numbers arrive every week. If scanner panel data are added to these market level data, and if about 60 summary calculations are reported with these data, the result would be over 800 million numbers, or about six million new numbers per week.

Chain Level Scanner Data. Assuming that there are five chains in each market and each chain only carries about 40% of the items in the category, the result is a database of about 540 million numbers, with 3.6 million new numbers arriving every Monday morning. Adding panel data to these data would result in about 1,500 million numbers or about 10 million new numbers per week.

Store Level Scanner Data. Assuming 14,000 stores carry 30% of the items in the category, the result is a database of 10,000 million numbers, or 10 billion numbers. About 70 million new numbers would arrive every week.

The numbers in the following table summarize the relative order of magnitude of a typical database in the various configurations:

Store audit	1 million
Warehouse withdrawal	10 million
Market level scanner	300 million
Chain level scanner	500 million
Store level scanner	10,000 million

Although these are "ball park" numbers that must be adjusted for the realities of any one category, they do indicate an enormous growth in the size of marketing databases. Brand groups could become overwhelmed with the data.

Consider a brand group that had been running its business with the old Nielsen data. They get 50,000 numbers every ninth week. Interviews with a number of these groups indicate that about five person-days would be devoted to analyzing these 50,000 numbers. This situation is not too bad: five days every ninth week.

This same group operating with the market level scanner data would receive two million numbers every week, a 40 times increase in the size of the data and a nine times increase in the frequency. Even if the group could become 40 times more efficient in their analysis, they would have to spend all the time analyzing the data. Just when they finished analyzing one week' s data, a new data set would arrive. Analysis paralysis has arrived.

A discussion with a manager who was installing a database on one frozen food category provides more insight into this situation. He reported the following dimensions: 10,000 UPCs, 45 markets, 20 measures, 150 weeks. Multiplying these figures would yield a hypothetical database of over one billion numbers. But data in categories like this are sparse due to the fact that not all UPCs are carried in each market or for all weeks. One way to think about the database is in terms of its " density," which refers to the fraction of the maximum numbers found in the actual database. A typical density is 25%, which would yield a database of 250 million numbers. The manager stated that storing the database required six gigabytes of disk space.

This data explosion means that the marketing managers have a difficult time capturing the opportunities in the data because of their sheer size. Data must be converted into information by applying marketing and analysis knowledge. This knowledge application process may break down because of the size of the databases.

Too Many Markets

A consumer market can be considered a geographical region encompassing at least one store. Data at finer levels of detail make it possible to analyze and market to increasingly smaller markets. The following chart shows typical regional breakdowns along with the number of resulting markets.

REGIONAL DEFINITION	NUMBER OF MARKETS
Nation	1
Nielsen regions	20
SAMI regions	50
Top 100 markets	100
ADI	200
Chains within ADI	1000
Stores	14000

Which of these levels is optimal? Although this question has not been answered, there is one development that may force firms to operate near the bottom of the table.

Just as the manufacturers of consumer goods are facing an opportunity derived from scanner data, the retailers face the same opportunity. These retail firms are beginning to realize that their data can also provide them with a means of gaining insight and competitive advantage. For instance, Jewel Foods reports that it has built an information system containing sales response models, which will allow its buyers and merchandisers to move from making merchandising decisions at the chain level to finer levels of geographical detail.

These parallel developments by retailers could serve to force the manufacturers to analyze at the same level as the major retailers. At the least, this move would result in the analysis of a chain within a market; at the maximum, it could even result in store-level analysis.

This move to finer granularity of the marketing effort calls for trade programs that take into consideration differences among retailers. In fact, there is some evidence that a change in the focus of marketing activities from the consumer to the customer is occurring. A recent magazine article highlights this trend:

> Which comes first, the retailer or the brand? In the most profound re-evaluation of brand management to date, many consumer-goods companies now say the retailer, and some are beginning to reorganize their marketing departments to prove it.[19]

This switch in emphasis is coming about because the retailers are making increasing demands on the manufacturers. Retailers are even demanding account specific promotions.[20] Manufacturers have to respond to these pressures by spending time and effort analyzing and understanding each account.

But the knowledge of different accounts is diffused among the managers in the field sales force. This diffusion is a barrier to the design of account and local marketing programs.

Too Few Resources

The problems presented by the magnitude of the data can be solved. The problem is not too few resources, it is the application of those resources. If marketing organizations are to overcome the barriers that face them and realize the opportunities that the scanner data have created, they must change along with the data. The next chapter describes the transitions that must take place.

NOTES

1. Dougherty, Philip H. "Market Research, At a Scan," *New York Times*, June 20, 1984.

2. Bermar, Amy. "Home-based TV Rating System: It Knows You' re Watching," *PC Week*, May 24, 1988, p. C/15.

3. Klokis, Holly. "Ukrop' s Tests Data Base Marketing Program," *Chain Store Age Executive*, September 1987, p. 73.

4. Coleman, Lynn. " 'Smart Card,' Coupon Eater Targeted to Grocery Retailers," *Marketing News*, June 6, 1988, p. 1.

5. Steinberg, Don. "Supermarket Offers Retailers ATM Funds Network Services," *PC Week*, October 27, 1987, p. C/9.

6. Lodish, Leonard M. *The Advertising & Promotion Challenge*, New York: Oxford University Press, 1986, p. 160.

7. Blattberg, Robert C., and Kenneth J. Wisniewski. "Price-Induced Patterns of Competition," Working Paper, Graduate School of Business, University of Chicago, 1986.

8. Wittink, Dick R., Michael J. Addona, William J. Hawkes, and John C. Porter. "SCAN*PRO: A Model to Measure Short-Term Effects of Promotional Activities on Brand Sales, Based on Store-Level Scanner Data," Working Paper, 1987.

9. Guadagni, Peter M., and John D. C. Little. "A Logit Model of Brand Choice Calibrated on Scanner Data," *Marketing Science*, 2 (Summer), pp. 203-38, 1983.

10. McAlister, Leigh. "The Impact of Price Promotions on a Brand' s Market Share, Sales Pattern, and Profitability," Marketing Science Institute Report No. 86-110, 1986.

11. Blattberg, Robert C., and Alan Levin. "Modelling the Effectiveness and Profitability of Trade Promotions," *Marketing Science* 6(Spring), 1987, pp. 124-46.

12. Klein, Robert L. "Using Supermarket Scanner Panels to Measure the Effectiveness of Coupon Promotions," in John Keon (Ed.), *Proceedings: Third ORSA/TIMS Special Interest Conference on Market Measurement and Analysis*, Providence, RI: The Institute of Management Sciences, 1981, pp. 118-26.

13. Toffler, Alvin. *The Third Wave*, New York: Morrow, 1980.

14. McCann, John. *The Marketing Workbench*, Homewood, IL: Dow Jones-Irwin, 1986.

15. Donahue, Christine. "Campbell Soup May Restructure in Favor of Regional Marketing," *Marketing Week*, May 4, 1987.

16. Lawrence, Jennifer. "Frito Play: New 'Basics' Strategy Takes on Regional Rivals," *Advertising Age*, March 30, 1987.

17. Freeman, Laurie. "P&G Hops on Regional Trend," *Advertising Age*, April 20, 1987.

18. Dagnoli, Judann. "Local Move: GF Prepares Regional Plan with Promo $," *Advertising Age*, February 9, 1987.

19. Donahue, Christine, and David Kiley. "Marketers to Focus on Retailer," *Adweek' s Marketing Week*, June 8, 1987, p. 1.

20. Petrison, Lisa. "Aiming the Pitch at the Corner Store," *Adweek' s Marketing Week*, September 21, 1987, p. 6.

CHAPTER 2

A NECESSARY TRANSITION

In creating opportunities, changes often demand new ways of thinking. This chapter describes the ways that marketing managers think about information systems today, and the ways their thinking must change to realize the opportunities offered by the data explosion.

THE NEW QUESTION

Managers know how to use their existing information systems. Once a system has been in place for a year or two, brand groups are probably using it the optimal level. They have intuitively measured the benefits and costs of the system, and have settled on a usage pattern that is best for them. Hence, the transition to higher usage will involve adding value to the system. This value will come through the data explosion. The new data and systems make possible an entirely new set of questions.

   The current situation is not so much a function of the systems as it is of the data. The older store-audit and warehouse withdrawal data are so aggregated and arrived so late that they are not "actionable." They serve primarily as a report card, allowing managers to measure their brands' actual performance versus the plan. Given the nature of the data, it is not surprising that marketing managers do not make extensive use of the existing systems.

   The Marketing Workbench listed several tasks that a typical brand group would like to perform using the marketing system:

- Examine on-deal cannibalization among your own brands and competitors.

- Design and monitor ad tests to maximize advertising effectiveness.

- Examine differences in regional response to advertising.

- Defend ad budgets intelligently or allocate to other needs.

- Monitor relative price movement for your brand to spot competitive changes.
- Analyze the profitability of price changes.
- Develop realistic test-market objectives using past test data more effectively.
- Prepare more accurate long-run forecasts with only three to six months of test market data.
- Diagnose sales results based on measures of consumer attitudes and behavior.
- Determine the impact of alternative marketing plans.

The problem is that report cards from the current marketing information systems do not help managers with these tasks.

Initial insight was provided by teaching an MBA course in Marketing Analysis. The students were given a " live" database containing Nielsen store audit data, SAMI warehouse withdrawal data, and shipment data. Playing the role of brand managers, they used a typical marketing information system, Acustar, to analyze the data. After five weeks of work, it became obvious that the data and system were not helping them make marketing decisions. Report cards answer the question, How' s business?

A better question is, What' s driving my business? While a report card is valuable, added value in the new systems will come from expanding it to answer this new question. The new integrated databases allow a manager to understand the causes of the results he sees in the report card.

Getting managers to ask this new question is easy; they already want its answer. But from an organizational and systems perspective, the transition is not so easy because today' s systems answer the old, How' s business? question; they do not contain the answer to the new, What' s driving my business? question.

COMPUTERIZATION

The data explosion is actually the second wave of new data to change the consumer goods industry. The first wave started with Nielsen' s store audit data service and advanced through the collection of warehouse withdrawal data by SAMI. These data allowed a transition from purely intuition-based marketing to data-based marketing.

Prior to these data, managers had to base marketing decisions on intuition because they lacked information on the performance of their brands in the market. The Nielsen and SAMI data gave them the ability to gain this understanding. The result was a period of computerization of the brand groups so that they could get answers to the question, How' s business?

Marketing managers used their new computer systems to learn about the market share, unit volume, dollar volume, and Brand Development Index (BDI) of their brands' business in multiple markets. They asked questions like, How are one-pound Folger cans doing in Boston in terms of unit sales, percent change versus a year ago, and BDI?

But, managers could not get valid and reliable answers to a more insightful question, What's driving my business? The second wave of data - the data explosion - provides the necessary causal factors to allow managers to ask and answer questions like, How much of our weekly 1986 volume of one-pound Folger's cans in Boston was due to our retail prices, our store displays, and our retail ad features?

The old computer systems only had to extract the appropriate data and make simple calculations on it. The manager used the computer to view the interesting portion of the database. Hence the term " data-based marketing."

But the answer to the What's driving my business? question is not in the database; it must be inferred from the data by models. If these models were available to the marketing manager and if they were put into a form that the typical manager could understand and use, then the practice of marketing could move to another level, model-based marketing.

Chapter 2 indicated that the models to support the transition from the How's business? to What's driving our business? have already been developed by market researchers. Given this history, a firm can legitimately ask the following question:

So, what's the big deal? We've got people who can do this modeling. And, we can always get our data supplier or an outside consulting firm to do it for us. We have been doing these studies for years; we call them Elasticity Studies; we've got drawers full of these reports.

The answer lies in the question itself: The problem has moved from an occasional study and report to a " big deal." These models will become so important that they will be the drivers of the marketing systems; the models will allow one to move from the existing marketing information systems to long-sought but elusive marketing decision support systems.

Marketing databases will grow to 1 million numbers with the Nielsen store audit data to 10 million numbers with the SAMI warehouse data to 300 million numbers with the market-level scanner data. Given this amount of data, a typical product category could require about 100,000 models and 2 million elasticities. Clearly, a systems problem exists. Marketing systems must evolve to include the management of models as well as data. The models can no longer be stuffed into drawers.

How will these models get built? Who will do the work? In today's environment, there are two existing approaches:

1. Marketing research professionals are commissioned, on a periodic basis, to build a set of models to answer a specific question.

2. An Assistant Product Manager (APM) will use the regression capabilities in the Marketing Management Information System (MMIS) to build regression models.

Marketing managers get either a series of ad hoc studies or an occasional model-building exercise by a recent MBA graduate.

Using the first approach, the ad hoc study, a problem is identified, a study is commissioned, and a report is prepared. This report is used to solve the problem, and it is then filed for later reference. The models do not become a part of the MMIS, and are not readily available and usable when needed.

The second approach, model development by an APM, is dangerous. Past experience in teaching MBA students indicates that they can grasp and apply the fundamentals of modeling during a semester course. But they seem to forget how to do the modeling after leaving school. This in not surprising since modeling is both a skill and an art requiring the education and experience of a professional. A firm should not place reliance on models that were formulated, estimated, and applied by an APM.

The need for a very large number of models that can be used by a manager at any point calls for the modeling process to be automated so that the model building becomes part of the maintenance of the marketing decision support system. The models must be available and on-line when the manager needs them to help answer a question or make a decision. Their development cannot wait for a special study when the problem becomes apparent.

Professional modelers (the word *marketmetricians* seems to describe these professionals) must be responsible for developing the model base. This development process involves an iterative process of model formulation, model estimation, and model criticism. The marketmetrician will play a major role because he or she is potentially responsible for millions of models. This issue is a " big deal."

In order move from a data focus to a models focus, marketing systems need to evolve beyond their current state as pure information processors. This section discusses such an evolution in terms of eras of marketing systems. The first two eras can be observed in firms today. Eras three and four will arise as firms begin to realize the power of the data explosion.

ERA I: VIEWING

Era I systems provide on-line access to internal shipment data as well as external data purchased from vendors such as A. C. Nielsen and SAMI/Burke. Such computerized access provide three primary benefits over the same information in hard copy: more timely access to the data, ability to view the data in new ways, and ability to dynamically define the data view. This computerized access led to the ability of managers to spot and understand problems. They do this spotting by viewing the data in new and different ways. Hence, we can call this era the *data viewing* era.

A company entered Era I when it made computerized market data available to marketing managers. The initial adoption of a computerized marketing information system was usually driven by either a very proactive marketing manager or by the marketing research organization. In the 1960s, a number of companies provided access to internal shipment data via a terminal tied to a mainframe. During the 1970s, the system was expanded to include data purchased from external sources: Nielsen store audit or SAMI warehouse withdrawal data.

The users of Era I information systems are either the marketing managers or the marketing researchers. Facilities for using the system tend to be centralized and relatively scarce. Small rooms are usually established with terminals linked to the corporate mainframe or an outside vendor' s computer. Era I usage focuses on spotting problems by comparing results in each area with its expected or planned value. Actual sales significantly below the planned level would indicate a problem.

Problems are also detected by comparing the actual results in one area with results in another. The other area serves as the standard of comparison. The area does not have to be just a geographic area. These comparisons could be made across time, across brands, or across markets.

A third way, closely related to the second way, is to build the standard into the measure. The Brand Development Index is a good example of this approach:

$$BDI = \dfrac{\dfrac{\text{Sales in a region}}{\text{Population in that region}}}{\dfrac{\text{Sales in the U.S.}}{\text{Population in the U.S.}}} \times 100$$

A BDI less than 100 indicates that the per capita sales in that region are below the U.S. average.

This type of analysis can be viewed as being a series of contrasts or "trolls" through the data. The manager is fishing or trolling for problems or opportunities. The standard in one troll may be different from that in another. In fact, the actual measure in one troll can become the standard in the next one.

For example, a troll could examine sales at the regional level; the per capita sales in each region (the actual measure) is compared with the U.S. average (the standard measure for this troll). After a particular problem region has been identified via this troll, the analysis is repeated by going deeper into that problem region. Per capita sales in each of the region's districts become the actual measure for the next troll, and per capita sales in that region could be used as the standard. Or, this district level analysis could use the U.S. sales levels as the standard instead of the region's sales levels. Keeping the same standard from one troll to another may be a better way to identify the core of the problem.

An important contrast in trolling is the difference between problems and opportunities. During the firm's planning process, managers commit their function to achieving a certain result or level of performance. If actual performance falls below the committed level, then there is a problem. Top-down problem detection involves the comparison of these high-level performance measures with the promised level; when performance falls short, managers start to troll for those performance elements that are causing the top-line number to be out of whack. They are trying to locate the source of the problem.

This approach contrasts with a bottom-up approach. With this approach managers take a perspective that says that although they may be on target with respect to their total performance levels, there are probably some areas in which they can improve. Some markets/brand-items are doing better than average, and others are below average. In this case, managers go directly to the lower levels of the brand-item and market hierarchies to those items or markets that are below expectation. These areas present opportunities to improve and exceed the promised performance levels.

Alternatively, the bottom-up approach can be conducted in a slightly different manner. Instead of searching for brand-items and markets that are below average, a manager can search for those that are above average. Once these high-performance situations are detected, a manager can go to causal analysis to gain an understanding of why they achieved the result. Given this understanding of the causal factors, which seem to lead to good performance, the manager can then examine the problem areas and compare the levels of the causal factors in the high performance areas and the low performance areas. The goal is the detection of those elements of the marketing mix which are working, and then to determine if these elements can be transported into the low-performance areas.

Era I systems have changed the way companies think about marketing. Use of the systems have given managers a new understanding of the variation in performance levels in different regions of the country. This understanding has lead to an increased emphasis on regional marketing efforts. It has also lead to an increased understanding of the impact of promotions on share and volume. The result is local focus marketing and a reliance on trade rather than consumer promotions. Later eras promise even greater changes.

ERA II: ANALYZING

The second era began in late 1986 and is characterized by several important features and developments.

Mergers

In 1980, the marketing information industry was characterized by multiple data vendors and separate software vendors. Each vendor had a piece of the total data available. Given the different sources of the data, the software vendors developed systems that would take any and all data, resulting in very general software that did not contain intelligence about the data. This software was a tool with which the manager could design and produce reports, and perform rudimentary analyses. In the early-to-mid part of this decade, the software and data vendors went on a merger spree, and there is no reason to believe that the end is in sight. The goal seems obvious: a single-source supplier of software and data for use by marketing and sales managers.

The combination of the software developer and the integrated database vendor makes it possible to put considerable knowledge about the data into the software. This permits the software to move from a tool to a solution package; from a system that the manager can use to obtain information useful in solving a problem to a system that solves problems.

Integrated Data

The new data integrates data from several sources: scanners, store-audits, advertising monitoring, coupon redemption, and scanner-panels. This results in a database containing data on variables such as:

units	repeat
distribution	ad feature
price	depth of repeat
trial	coupons
display	inter-purchase time

Era I databases tend to contain only outcome or results data (units, cases, distribution). Era II databases contain data on factors that may cause the result measure to change.

These integrated data allow the manager to move from problem and opportunity identification to analysis of the factors that caused the problems and opportunities.

PC-based Software

The hardware changed as the data and software changed. Era I software was designed to be used via a terminal tied to a mainframe. When the manager wanted to access the mainframe from a PC, additional software and hardware were added to make the PC perform like a terminal. Era II software takes advantage of the unique features of the PC: quick screens, rapid response, graphics, and fast retrieval from small datasets. These features have resulted in software that is easier to use. The ease of use is primarily due to designs that require the manager to remember almost nothing about the software or the product category under study. Menus and icons remind him of the available selections.

MIS Joins the Battle

Even the strategic value of the information systems changed with the addition of the new data. During Era I, the Management Information Systems (MIS) managers thought of their jobs as providing a service for marketing managers. During Era II, the emphasis has shifted to the question: How can MIS provide a strategic, competitive advantage via the application of information and information technology to our sales and marketing functions?

This shift has had a very significant impact: It has brought more resources to bear on the computerization of marketing and sales. Computers are no longer being looked at as a means for increasing the efficiency of marketing managers. They are viewed as a competitive weapon, alongside other weapons such as promotion and advertising.

Retailer Involvement

The retailers are beginning to recognize that they can improve their profitability through the collection and analysis of information. Retailers who installed scanners in their stores did so to reduce labor costs. Having achieved this objective, they have turned their attention to increasing profit through better merchandising decisions.

Retailers have seen that they can improve their buying and merchandising decisions through the use of the new data and technology. This new awareness is changing the buyer/seller relationships between retailer and manufacturer because the buyer can make more informed decisions. The result is a channel power shift towards the retailer caused by the existence of information in the hands of the retail decision makers.

From Viewing Data to Analyzing Data

One of the most important aspects of the transition from Era I to Era II is the shift from the practice of problem spotting-and-bounding to an analysis of the causal factors that led to the problem. Companies have always wanted to know the causes of problems but they have been unable to find them because the old data lacks the level of detail needed to get that information. The new integrated databases contain the necessary data, and the weekly periodicity of the data make it possible to observe the interrelationship between the performance measures and the pattern of marketing mix elements.

Marketing research professionals are building models that capture the following types of causal relationships:

the impact of the marketing mix elements on brand sales and shares

the competitive structure within a category

the lead/lag relationships between share and the individual mix elements such as price and advertising

Firms will develop standard models and methodologies for providing these types of analyses. The output will be a set of models and coefficients for different brand items in different markets. It will be possible to obtain estimates of the impact of each marketing mix measure on each brand-item in each market. If the data contain 10 measures on each of 1000 items in 100 markets, the result will be 1 million coefficients and 100,000 models.

ERA III: SYNTHESIZING

Era III will be a period of understanding and synthesis of the implications of the causal models and structures that evolved during Era II. Era III systems will be devoted to "bringing the models alive" for the managers. These managers will use the system to understand their markets. This new understanding will be a model-based understanding, as opposed to a direct understanding of the actual market from looking at data.

Managers who have 1 million coefficients may have been dealing with 150 million numbers in the Era I data-focused world. So, they go from being buried in millions of numbers to being buried in thousands of models, a more manageable problem. Perhaps more importantly, the information will be much more valuable. When managers use the models to look at historical performance, they will be able to determine why the market share changed. Why did share go down in the Northeast and rise in the South? When managers use the models to look forward, they will be able to estimate the impact of future marketing mix designs on brand performance.

But managers have also moved into an unknown world of models and elasticities. They were comfortable with any one of the 150 million numbers in the Era I system because they represented concepts with which they had experience. A number that measures the units of Tide sold in Omaha during the week of December refers to a concept (unit sales) about which managers have a real-world counterpart. If the information system reported that those numbers were going down, or that they were higher in New England than in Texas, everyone knows the meaning of this fact.

When the number stands for a coefficient of a variable in a model, managers are dealing with something that does not have a real-world counterpoint. They must gain an understanding of the concepts underlying the models before they will accept the implications of the models. And they must be able to communicate these implications in terms that most people in the firm can understand.

This Era III synthesis has already occurred at some levels with the introduction of Lotus 1-2-3. Managers could understand how large mainframe models worked. But they were not able to routinely use the results of the models in their daily work. They were not able to internalize the models.

But when brand groups were given an electronic spreadsheet, the situation changed. They would put the models into the spreadsheet, and then perform a simulation by varying the inputs and graphing the performance of the outputs. They would treat the model as a " black box." In this way, they were able to deal with familiar concepts: patterns of numbers and graphs. They would be able to graph the input numbers along with the output numbers and graphically see the causal relations. Although they could have directly examined the models themselves, they were better able to internalize the relationship by looking at the numerical and graphical results.

Era III systems will be devoted to bringing the model bases alive for the managers. These managers will use the system to gain a whole new understanding of their markets. This new understanding will be a model-based understanding, as opposed to a direct understanding of the actual market gained by looking at data about that market. This reliance on a model representation of the markets rather than the markets themselves is necessary because the managers want to understand the relationships in the markets.

ERA IV: DESIGNING

Once managers have become comfortable with using model-based representations of the world, they are ready to move to the next stage: using the model as a guide to the design of a marketing program. By looking over the past few years, they will be able to understand the forces that had been driving the business. This understanding will lead to the design of a new marketing mix, and Era IV systems will assist in such design. These systems can also be used to ascertain the probable impact of this new program on the brand's performance.

The challenge for the system designer is to make this system as intelligent as possible, to make it a friendly design advisor. The role models for such systems can be found in systems developed to assist the designer of mechanical and electronic parts. These systems use a principle of designing by customizing existing elements. For instance, if a manager wants to design a coupon, the computer presents a screen or window that contains slots for specifying each attribute of the coupon. The new coupon is designed by customizing these elements for the current situation.

An architecture for designing by customizing existing elements evolved during the early 1980s in the development of engineering-oriented workstations.[1] In this architecture, the workstation screen contains icons that represent the elements that will compose the design. A generic frame is attached to each icon, which contains rules, knowledge, programs, and pointers to other frames and programs that pertain to the element being represented by the icon. This frame might contain the basic template of a coupon or a Plan-o-gram.

If the manager wants to design a coupon program and see how it will play, he picks the Coupon Generic Frame and customizes it with the specifics of his program. The system will know what task the manager is performing and will automatically bring up the data he should be considering. For instance, a Generic Frame for a mail coupon may have a slot for Value and may contain some rules or knowledge about the most appropriate value under certain sets of circumstances. The Generic Frame would use predefined rules and past history to suggest an optimum value for the slot. The manager could override that suggestion if he knows of special circumstances that affect this particular coupon. This workbench should provide for automatic access to the MMIS to get the past history.

The design of any promotion program would benefit from this approach, because in general it is an iterative process in which the manager

1) uses the MMIS to perform an analysis of the brand's situation,

2) uses this situation assessment to devise a promotion strategy,

3) selects a set of promotion devices or elements that are thought to be appropriate for the selected strategy,

4) ascertains the degree to which these elements are able to "operationalize" the strategy and correct or solve the situation, and

5) cycles through these steps until a final design is produced.

The following scenario provides an initial view of such a design workbench. The manager sits down at the computer screen. She selects the icon that denotes "Develop a Promotion Strategy." Then she selects other icons for the brand and the market. The computer then flips her into a new screen that could contain a dialogue with a knowledge-based system running on a mainframe. This screen asks some questions, accesses the database for the correct Brand Profile, and recommends a strategy. The system then takes the next step of using another knowledge-based system to select those promotional elements or devices which are appropriate for this strategy, brand, and market.

If the manager indicates that she wants to design a promotional event, the system displays the icons that correspond to those elements that are appropriate for inclusion in the event. And, it flips her into the Promotion Design mode by providing a design area on the screen, along with the promotion elements icons.

The manager then selects the desired elements and moves them into the design area. The system fires up another knowledge-based system, which looks at the collection of elements and offers any advice about adding or dropping elements.

When a tentative design is completed, the system simulates the success of the promotion utilizing the model base. The manager can then use this simulator to ask "what if" questions or perform a simulation on the impact of other events on the brand's performance. She may be considering intangible variables such as brand franchise, but wants to see what the tangible cost will be if she considers it.

This type of workbench begins to assume some of the characteristics of a Knowledge Medium.[2] A Knowledge Medium is a set of programs that enhance an individual's ability to apply knowledge to a problem. Managers need this kind of help from the computer. John Little described the typical manager's approach to using a computer:

> *Managers do not like terminals. They are impatient and busy. They do not formulate problems in model terms because that is not the way they actually think. They want to think about strategy, not analysis. They will propose actions to be analyzed, but they will not do it themselves.*[3]

The Knowledge Medium structures the analysis based on the managers suggestions. This vision of the marketing workstation in 1990 requires us to move away from the phrase *Marketing Management Information System* (MMIS) because it focuses on information. An information system provides computerized access to information. But, managers will have too much information to spend their time accessing.

Further, the tired phrase *Decision Support System* (DSS) has a confused image. To some, it is nothing more than an information system. To most proponents, it is the extension of an information system into a modeling system. To most computer users, it is a just confusing phrase.

The phrase *Computer Assisted Marketing* (CAM) focuses on the activity facing most marketing managers: marketing. It moves the focus from information to decisions to marketing. In this world of CAM, a manager uses the workstation to do marketing, not to do data analysis.

Marketing can be defined as understanding and influencing a market via the marketing mix. Focus on MMIS and DSS usually involves the first component of marketing: understanding a market. If this understanding is in the computer, the manager can shift the focus to the design of marketing programs for influencing markets.

SUMMARY

The four eras can be summarized by comparing them in four ways: emphasis, focus, exploding, and managing.

Emphasis: What types of questions will managers use the system to answer?

Focus: What will the firm be focusing on as it deals with the issues that arise in using the system?

Exploding: As managers use the system in each era, certain aspects of their work will be growing very rapidly.

Managing: From a marketing management perspective, what skills will be required to manage the key aspect of the system and its output?

Era I systems are used primarily to view marketing data. Hence the following can be said about each aspect:

Emphasis: What happened to what brands in what markets during what time periods?
Focus: Data
Exploding: Data
Managing: Data overload

This is clearly a data viewing era in which managers finally get their long-sought wish: *just let me have computer access to my data in an easy-to-use form*. They can thus learn the status of all brand items in all markets on a weekly basis.

This era will occur in most firms during the 1980s. During this period, database size will go from dozens of megabytes to hundreds of megabytes to gigabytes and perhaps even terabytes. Dealing with these databases will require a large amount of the time of the MIS and marketing services departments.

Marketing managers will have to learn to do marketing in an environment of data overload. The successful Era I systems allow the manager to gain easy access to the data.

Era II will be entered when the firm recognizes that it should be answering the question, What's driving my business? This era has the following characteristics:

Emphasis: What were the causes?
Focus: Modeling
Exploding: Models
Managing: Technical modeling

Era II systems will be used to produce the models that explain the Era I results. The focus will be on the modeling process and the result will be a rapid increase in the number of models. This technical modeling must be managed by the firm.

Era III arrives when the firm has produced or acquired a set of models, producing the following characteristics:

Emphasis: What do I know?
Focus: models
Exploding: understanding
Managing: complexity

Era III systems are designed to bring alive the models so that managers can understand their meaning and implications.

The result will be a sharp rise in the level of understanding of the factors and forces that are driving their business. Firms will have to learn how to manage the marketing function in an environment where they have a deeper understanding of the impacts of most of their actions on brand performance.

Era IV promises to be an era where the marketer can move beyond data, modeling, and models to focus on the world of marketing. This era will have the following characteristics:

Emphasis: What do I do?
Focus: Consumers, competitors, trade
Exploding: marketing
Managing: marketing

A successful Era IV system will improve the efficiency and effectiveness of managers as they design marketing programs. This increased effectiveness will allow managers to understand and influence many more markets than is possible in an Era I world. The result will be an explosion in the amount of marketing an individual manager can accomplish.

In conclusion, marketing systems need to evolve from data viewing systems to modeling systems to model viewing systems to marketing design systems. This evolution has to take place in an environment where there are far too much data and too many models for the firm to continue to utilize labor intensive systems.

The transition from Era I to Eras II and III can be seen as an evolutionary process in which systems and organizations must be put in place to manage this evolutionary process. The Marketing Workbench Laboratory serves as a catalyst and change agent. The Lab will articulate the needs, explain what is possible, build prototypes of new systems, work with software developers on the transition of our prototypes into finished products, and conduct educational programs to distribute the results of this research.

The next section describes the knowledge-based systems that will be the basis for these new marketing information systems.

NOTES

1. Rauch-Hindin, Wendy B. *Artificial Intelligence in Business, Science, and Industry: Volume I: Fundamentals*, Englewood Cliffs: Prentice-Hall, 1985, pp. 113-128.

2. Stefik, Mark. " The Next Knowledge Medium," *The AI Magazine*, Vol 7, No. 1, Spring 1986, pp. 34-46.

3. Little, John D. C. " Decision Support Systems for Marketing Managers," *Journal of Marketing*, Vol. 43, Summer 1979, p. 22.

SECTION II:

KNOWLEDGE-BASED SYSTEMS

CHAPTER 3

AN INTRODUCTION TO KNOWLEDGE SYSTEMS[1]

This chapter provides an overview of knowledge system technology. Knowledge systems are a new *class* of computer application, as are spreadsheets, data management systems, and word processors. Each has a set of tasks for which it is appropriate. The tools are designed specifically to address the requirements of these tasks.

For example, spreadsheets have an underlying structure for dealing with quantitative modeling. Fundamental elements in this type of tool are *cells* and the linkages among them. Spreadsheets allow various types of information to be placed in these cells. They provide a syntax for describing the linkages, and many features and functions to facilitate entering and editing these types of information.

Word processors are designed for representing, manipulating and formatting text. Underlying concepts here are letters, words, paragraphs, etc. The tool is designed to facilitate the editing and formatting of these units of text material.

As a class of computer application, knowledge system development tools are also based on an underlying model of their task. Instead of cells and linkages, or words and sentences, they are designed to manage such task components as *rules* and *inferencing*. Specific knowledge system development tools have similarities as a class of applications, as well as tool-to-tool variance. In this chapter, the subject of knowledge systems will be introduced with the objective of clarifying the similarities that define them as a class of tool. Differences among specific tools are not discussed.

Before beginning, it may be useful to briefly clarify some terminology. In particular, it may be useful to articulate what is meant by such terms as *artificial intelligence*, *expert systems*, and *knowledge-based systems*.

Artificial intelligence is an area of research and development generally associated with the disciplines of computer science and psychology. In its most general sense, artificial intelligence is concerned with creating computer programs that exhibit "intelligent" behavior. Here, "intelligent," generally meant that the program solves problems by applying knowledge and reasoning that mimics human problem solving. To make machines more intelligent, researchers often study human problem solvers. Artificial intelligence is a broad term that addresses such diverse topics as speech comprehension and robotic vision systems.

One of the earliest techniques for creating intelligent programs was the expert system approach. As the name implies, expert systems have focused on modeling the reasoning, or problem-solving behavior of experts in some specific area. Later, as the techniques became more generalizable, the label "expert" became problematic because of its seemingly restrictive application to true "expertise." When these same programming technologies are applied to model reasoning of a less rare and lofty status, they are referred to as knowledge systems. The technologies are the same, the quality or rarity of the knowledge being modeled provides the distinction. The label *knowledge* system is somewhat more general and useful than *expert* system; however, the early establishment of the term *expert* system makes it a resistant incumbent, and the terms ore often used interchangeably.

In developing expert systems, early artificial intelligence researchers focused on two tasks of primary importance to the field:

1. Finding effective, generalizable methods for *representing* knowledge so that it can be used by a computer, and

2. Developing effective, generalizable methods for computerized *reasoning* with this knowledge.

The result has been a class of tools for modeling knowledge and reasoning that *do not require the developer to be versed in the underlying theories and concepts of artificial intelligence.*

THE SEPARATION OF KNOWLEDGE AND REASONING

One of the features of knowledge systems is the separation of knowledge from the methods for reasoning with that knowledge. Knowledge system development tools provide a structure for representing knowledge and provide methods for reasoning with this knowledge. The user supplies the knowledge for the system and controls the reasoning process.

Two knowledge representation schemes have dominated knowledge system development tools: simple rule-based schemes and frame-based schemes. Of these, the simple rule-based are more common. They have proven to be easy for end-users to learn, and they are applicable to a class of applications resistant to traditional computing methods.

The rules in rule-based systems have an IF...THEN form. This IF...THEN form of rules appears similar to conditional statements in more traditional, procedural languages. However, the role the statements play and the way they are processed are quite different. Each rule is a modular element of knowledge. That is, each rule can be thought of as a chunk of knowledge. For example, a marketing manager may believe the following " chunk" of knowledge to be true:

If the product I am trying to market is one for which multiple purchases will lock consumers out of the market, and one for which the consumer will use more if they have more in their pantry, then I should try to promote the product by providing an incentive for the consumer to purchase several units at one time.

The phrase "multiple purchases lock consumers out of the market," simply means that if someone buys a lot of the product, they will not buy more until it is consumed. This locking out of the market makes the consumer resistant to incentives to buy similar products from other suppliers who may offer promotional schemes of their own.

An example product for which consumers will use more if they have more in the pantry is soft drinks. A product that does not have this characteristic is toothpaste. If consumers have several tubes, they still brush their teeth with the same amount of paste. This phenomenon is called "inventory and use correlation."

When this chunk of marketing knowledge is represented in a rule-based knowledge system, it can be translated to the following form:

```
If multiple-purchase-lock-out = true
and inventory-use-correlation = true
then promotion-strategy = convenience-purchasing.
```

The process of transforming knowledge that exists in the first, narrative form into the proper rule syntax of a particular knowledge-based development tool is an important part of the larger skill of knowledge engineering.

When several chunks of knowledge relevant for solving a particular class of problem have been converted to rules of the proper syntax, and these rules are combined with some other components discussed later, they form a knowledge base in a rule-oriented system.

√ Figure 3.1 contains a small, and intentionally trivial knowledge base for deciding among various places to advertise a product or event. The purpose of this example is simply to provide a context for describing just how rule-based systems reason with these chunks of knowledge. Each element of this knowledge base is labeled for easy reference as kb-1, through kb-10 (knowledge base entry 1 through knowledge base entry 10). The knowledge base in figure 3.1 conforms to the conventions of a particular knowledge system development tool, M.1, from Teknowledge, Inc. While this knowledge base is written in the syntax of that specific tool, the fundamental qualities of rule-based systems described below are generic to that entire class of tools.

It is important to note at this point that what is depicted in figure 3.1 is actually what the developer must supply. While, in this trivial example, the quality of the knowledge is questionable and hardly complete, this is the nature of what the developer must supply.

```
kb-1: goal = where-to-advertise

kb-2: if product-category = liquor
      or product-category = tobacco
      then media = print

kb-3: if product-category = automobile
      then media = television

kb-4: if product-category = local-event
      then media = radio

kb-5: if media = print and
      status-of-target-market = upscale
      then where-to-advertise = 'Gourmet Magazine'

kb-6: if media = print and
      status-of-target-market = middle-income
      then where-to-advertise = 'Time Magazine' cf 80

kb-7: if media = television and
      age-of-target-market = children
      then where-to-advertise = 'Saturday Morning Cartoons'

kb-8: if media = television and
      age-of-target-market = middle-age
      then where-to-advertise = 'Johnny Carson Show'

kb-9: if media = radio and
      age-of-target-market = youth
      then where-to-advertise = 'Rock Radio'

kb-10: if media = radio and
       age-of-target-market = senior-citizens
       then where-to-advertise = 'Easy Listening Radio'
```

Figure 3.1. Sample Knowledge Base for Deciding Among Advertising Campaign Options

In figure 3.2, two sample runs of this knowledge base with the M.1 system are provided to give a flavor of a typical user-system interaction. In fairness to the developers of M.1, it should be noted that a completed knowledge base would contain additional instructions to further enhance screen formats, and generally pretty up the interaction. In the context of this discussion, it would simply confuse the issue to add the additional formatting instructions to the knowledge base.

```
Dialog 1

> go

What is the value of: product-category?

> local-event

> What is the value of: age-of-target-market

> senior-citizen

> where-to-advertise = Easy Listening Radio (100%)
  because of kb-10


Dialog 2

> go

> What is the value of: product-category?

> tobacco

> What is the value of: status-of-target-market?

> upscale

> where-to-advertise = Gourmet Magazine (100%)
  because of kb-5
```

Figure 3.2. Sample Dialogs with the Knowledge Base in Figure 3.1

Most personal computer users are comfortable with placing algebraic knowledge into a spreadsheet in the form of numbers, labels, and equations. The knowledge base in figure 3.1 and spreadsheets are analogous in that the end-user is not supplying information about *how* the model is to be processed by the tool. In both cases, the knowledge bases and spreadsheets are acted upon by their tools. A spreadsheet processes the contents of its cells. While it is *possible* in Lotus 1-2-3 to alter the order in which functions and formulas are computed, this capability is infrequently used in practice. Similarly, it is *possible* to alter the process by which the knowledge base in figure 3.1 is processed by the M.1 tool. However, it is not necessary to do any more than type the word *go* for the default processing methods to be applied.

In this way, the representation of the knowledge and the processing of the knowledge are separated. The developer primarily focuses on the nature of the knowledge and the way it is represented. The tool developer has, to a large degree, provided the methodology for processing and applying this knowledge in solving specific problems. In more complex problem areas, it is desirable to have more flexibility and control over the processing of knowledge. Available tools vary considerably along this dimension.

THE INFERENCE PROCESS: BACKWARD CHAINING

Rule-based knowledge systems can generally be categorized as backward or forward chaining in the ways that they process knowledge bases. The more popular have been backward chaining inference systems. These have evolved from the famous MYCIN system. MYCIN was developed to perform medical diagnosis of infectious blood diseases. Its spin-off, EMYCIN, was one of the first attempts at a generalized knowledge system development tool. EMYCIN stands for Empty MYCIN. In EMYCIN, rules and methods for processing the rules were separated. This feature allowed the developer to simply remove the rules for medical diagnosis and insert rules appropriate for different applications, such as the advertising rules in the previous example.

This evolution from MYCIN to EMYCIN was an important development in the field of expert system research. It represented a generalization from a single application to an application development tool. Along with the separation of rules from reasoning, however, came another generalization. One of the primary characteristics of the original MYCIN program was the way in which it reasoned with these rules. This method of reasoning is known as backward chaining. As in the original MYCIN system, backward chaining systems are primarily useful in solving problems that are *diagnostic* in nature. Some of the literature refers to this type of problem as a structured selection problem. In essence, these problems are characterized by a set of solutions (diagnoses) that are enumerable and specifiable in advance. The objective of the system is to determine which of these prespecified choices is the correct one under the prevailing circumstances.

In the trivial example of figure 3.1, the problem is to select "where-to-advertise" from the choices provided. In many situations, the possible solutions to a particular type of problem can be enumerated in advance. Under different circumstances, different choices are appropriate. These selection, or diagnostic problems are well suited to backward chaining systems.

Again, the example knowledge base in figure 3.1 is intentionally trivial to illustrate the fundamental operating characteristics of the backward chaining inference technique. Normally, a knowledge base would also contain other types of information, which controls the flow of processing and formats the interaction with the user. Regardless of the presence or absence of these additional features, the basic process of drawing inferences is simple, and straightforward.

In backward chaining systems, the reasoning is always driven by a goal. In figure 3.1, kb-1 states "goal = where-to-advertise." The system will process the knowledge base until it achieves a value for this goal, or has tried every means at its disposal to do so.

By just examining the rules in figure 3.1, the reader *could* apply them to achieve a value for the goal of "where-to-advertise": In so doing, however, it would be found that other information would be needed. For example, there is no way to use the rules in figure 3.1 to conclude a value for "where-to-advertise" without first determining a value for "media." In turn, a value for "media" cannot be found without first determining a value for "product-category." It can also be seen that, depending upon the value that is found for "media," values must be found for either "status-of-target-market," or for "age-of-target-market." It is important that the reader confirm these statements by examining the knowledge base in figure 3.1.

The concept here is simply that in finding the value of one expression, in this case "where-to-advertise," the system will generally have to also seek the value of other expressions (e.g., "media," "product-category," and either "status-of-target-market," or "age-of-target-market"). During the process of finding a value for the goal of "where-to-advertise," that goal can be made dormant, or temporarily suspended, while the system seeks one of the subgoals (e.g., "media"). In an iterative fashion, each of these subgoals can also be suspended while the system seeks another subgoal (e.g., "product-category"). The setting of subgoals for other subgoals is an important capability of backward chaining rule-based systems.

When seeking the value for an expression, the system has several methods to apply. These methods are applied in a particular sequence. This sequence can be modified under user control, and to varying degrees with different tools. However, in their simplest form, backward chaining systems will follow this sequence of methods to find the value for a goal or subgoal:

Method 1: Check the system's temporary or working memory to see if a value for the goal or subgoal has already been found by some previous operation.

Method 2: Try to find a rule in the knowledge base that would be useful in determining a value for the goal or subgoal. Such a rule is called a relevant rule. The nature of relevant rules is described below.

Method 3: Ask the user for a value for the goal or subgoal.

If either method 2 or 3 result in a value for a goal or subgoal, that value is noted in working memory in case it is needed later in processing the knowledge base.

The finding of relevant rules is critical to understanding the nature of backward chaining. All rules are in the

```
IF premise THEN conclusion
```

format. A relevant rule is one for which the *conclusion* will result in a value for the current goal or subgoal being sought.

In order to clarify the nature of backward chaining, it will be helpful to walk through the knowledge base in figure 3.1, and see how Dialog 1 of figure 3.2 was generated. The reader should follow this description closely and verify the processing by referring to the relevant figures. This will result in a fundamentally greater understanding of the inferencing process than a casual review. To begin, the system *must* establish a goal. This goal is supplied by kb-1, which states:

```
goal = where-to-advertise.
```

Method 1 is tried, and, of course fails, because no value for the expression "where-to-advertise" has been found by a previous operation, and is not to be found in working memory. In fact, as the session has just begun, working memory is completely empty.

Applying method 2, the system begins looking for a relevant rule and finds kb-f:

```
if media = print and
status-of-target-market = upscale
then where-to-advertise = 'Gourmet Magazine.'
```

This rule is relevant because it concludes a value for the present goal. *Only after identifying a rule as relevant, is the premise of the rule examined.* Kb-f has as its premise:

```
If media = print and status-of-target-market = upscale
```

The first clause, *if media = print*, forces the system to establish a subgoal. The previous goal of "where-to-advertise" is made dormant, and "media" becomes the active subgoal.

At this point, the process begins anew, and the system applies methods 1—3, in sequence, for the newly established subgoal, "media." Again, method 1 fails. Method 2 results in a new relevant rule, kb-2:

```
if product-category = liquor
```

```
or product-category = tobacco
then media = print.
```

It is relevant because it concludes a value for " media," the currently active subgoal. Again, the premise of kb-2 is now, and only now, examined. Its premise:

```
if product-category = liquor or product-category = tobacco
```

results in the establishment of a new subgoal, " product-category," and the current subgoal of " media" is made dormant.

With a new subgoal, the system begins again by applying methods 1 through 3. Method 1 fails again. Method 2 also fails as there are no rules that conclude a value for " product-category." Method 3 is applied, and, as can be seen in Dialog 1 of figure 3.2, the system asks the user for the value of " product-category." The user responds that the value is " local-event."

At this point, the value of " product-category" is noted in working memory, and the current subgoal of " product-category" is eliminated, as its value has been found. The last-made dormant subgoal, " media" reawakens and becomes the system's active subgoal. Rule kb-2, which the system was working on when " media" became dormant, now can be tested. It fails because the required value of " product-category" is known to be inconsistent with the rule's premise.

The system continues applying method 2 in finding a value for " media" and finds another relevant rule in kb-3. The reader can see why this rule will fail, and subsequently, why rule kb-4 will succeed. Kb-4 is successful and fires. Its success results in a value for " media" placed in working memory. The long-dormant goal of " where-to-advertise" reawakens. When it does, rule kb-5 is re-tried, as the system was busy applying method 2, and looking at rule kb-5, when the goal was made dormant. The premise of kb-5 requires that the value of " media" be " radio," so kb-5 fails.

The process continues with " where-to-advertise" as the goal. Rules kb-6, kb-7, and kb-8 fail, in sequence, as the first clauses of their premises are false. However, when kb-9 is examined, it is also relevant. The first part of its premise is true; however, the second clause, " and age-of-target-market = youth," includes a new and unknown expression. The user should be able to see why Dialog 1 in figure 3.2 proceeds as it does, and how the final value of " where-to-advertise" is derived from the success of kb-10.

The point of this walk through the knowledge base is that the system works *backwards from conclusions to test premises* and does so in a recursive fashion through a simple algorithm. In short, the system applies simple methods, in a particular order, to draw inferences from the knowledge supplied by the user. The means by which inferences are drawn is called the system's "inference engine." In this case, the inference engine is of the " backward-chaining" type.

The processing required to create the simple, very short, interaction of Dialog 1 in figure 3.2, is considerable. However, the perseverance and consistency of the system in applying these inferencing methods is one of its significant strengths. Inference engines once were hand-coded for each knowledge system. However, this is an example of an off-the-shelf inference engine. The nature of the inference engine, its flexibility, and details of its operation are important characteristics of any knowledge system development tool.

DEALING WITH UNCERTAINTY

One of the often-discussed capabilities of knowledge systems is the ability to reason with uncertainty. Two concepts underlie this ability. The first is that of *certainty factors*, and the second is the set of *algorithms for combining certainty factors*. Figure 3.3 displays an identical knowledge base to that found in figure 3.1, with the exception that certainty factors have been added to the conclusions of several of the rules in the form " cf 70," where 70 indicates the level of certainty the developer has in the rule' s conclusion, on a scale of 0 to 100.

That is, the conclusion of kb-3, that the proper media for advertising automobiles is television has been hedged by the statement " cf 90," which follows the conclusion. This indicates that the developer is 90% certain that this conclusion would be correct. Similarly, kb-4 has been amended to draw two conclusions for the value of " media" under the conditions of its premise. Under these conditions, the system would conclude both that " radio" and " print" would be appropriate media for advertising, with certainty factors of 70 and 60 respectively. As one could be confident of both of these conclusions simultaneously, there is no need for them to " add" to 100, as with probabilities.

These simple hedges may appear straight forward at first glance; however, it can soon be seen that there are many opportunities for them to be combined, or accounted for, as the system gathers information from one rule and uses it to test the premises for later rules. For example, in figure 3.3, if kb-4 were to fire and the two conclusions for the value of media were stored in working memory, along with their certainty factors, how would this affect the processing of rules kb-5, kb-6, kb-9, and kb-10? Would their premises be found to be true? If so, how does this affect the system' s confidence in the conclusions of these rules?

This ability to work with uncertainty varies somewhat from tool to tool, but generally follows methods that have been handed down from the original MYCIN and EMYCIN systems. A more detailed description of how these methods operate is provided in the next chapter. For now, however, let it be made clear that the methodology for combining and/or weighting confidence in various sources of information *does not come from either probability theory or from bayesian statistics*. In some systems, the user has some control over the ways in which evidence for conclusions is combined and interpreted, in others, not. In some systems, users can apply *negative* certainty, that is, confidence that something can *not* be true. In others, this capability is not provided. However, all rule-based system development tools provide some methodology for reasoning with uncertain, or completely absent information.

Backward chaining systems, with their search for relevant chunks of knowledge are very effective in processing the modular rules that act as components of the knowledge base. It should be evident why this approach is so applicable to the broad class of diagnostic, or structured-selection problems.

```
kb-1: goal = where-to-advertise

kb-2: if product-category = liquor
      or product-category = tobacco
      then media = print

kb-3: if product-category = automobile
      then media = television cf 90

kb-4: if product-category = local-event
      then media = radio cf 70 and
      media = print cf 60

kb-5: if media = print and
      status-of-target-market = upscale
      then where-to-advertise = 'Gourmet Magazine' cf 60

kb-6: if media = print and
      status-of-target-market = middle-income
      then where-to-advertise = 'Time Magazine' cf 80

kb-7: if media = television and
      age-of-target-market = children
      then where-to-advertise = 'Saturday Morning Cartoons'

kb-8: if media = television and
      age-of-target-market = middle-age
      then where-to-advertise = 'Johnny Carson Show' cf 50

kb-9: if media = radio and
      age-of-target-market = youth
      then where-to-advertise = 'Rock Radio' cf 60

kb-10: if media = radio and
       age-of-target-market = senior-citizens
       then where-to-advertise = 'Easy Listening Radio'
```

Figure 3.3. Sample Knowledge Base with Certainty Factors

Backward chaining systems have been the most popular design for the first group of knowledge system development tools. There are several reasons. First, the technique has proven to be a successful one in numerous applications. Second, there are many applications that fit the approach very well and form an attractive set of application areas. Third, there are several commercial development packages based upon this model. Inference engines that are rule-based and backward chaining are relatively easy to code and deliver on mainstream hardware. Finally, the approach seems to be quite intuitive. Users who are unfamiliar with knowledge systems seem to grasp rather quickly just how their knowledge bases are being used by the inferencing system. This is a substantial factor in the demystification and acceptance of this technology.

THE INFERENCE PROCESS: FORWARD CHAINING

Rule-based systems can also use an inference technique known as *forward chaining* in place of, or in addition to, the *backward chaining* inference engine described above. This approach also has been generalized from several individually developed and proven applications. The most notable, and most often discussed forward chaining knowledge system application is the R1, or XCON system developed for the Digital Equipment Corporation (DEC). This system, an eXpert CONfiguration system, creates specific configurations of computer components from a large inventory of available parts to meet specific customer needs. DEC provides a large number of interactive components, which are assembled to produce a specific, unique system for an individual customer; the problem of identifying the proper components and assuring that their interaction will result in a working system is a difficult one.

They, like most other computer manufacturers, had encountered problems as sales representatives in the field, working with individual customers, specified system components that would sometimes turn out to be unworkable in combination, redundant in function, or unnecessary, or would fail to identify necessary components as part of the total configuration. As each order was entered, system engineers would have to begin the process of analyzing the order, and then refining it, or working out the bugs with the sales representative and customer. This process was time consuming, required highly trained and highly paid employees, and formed a bottleneck in the flow of products and services.

The XCON system was developed to configure the proper combination of components to do the job. It is most important to note that the *nature of the problem* for this system is not a diagnostic or structured selection problem. That is, it is not possible in advance to enumerate all of the possible configurations that could be constructed from the available components and then choose from this set. The combinatorial aspects of the problem simply make such an approach infeasible. The nature of this problem is *design* as opposed to *selection*.

Forward chaining inference procedures appear to be most applicable in this design process. The distinction between forward and backward chaining is a relatively simple one in terms of how the inferencing is done. The knowledge bases for the two approaches need not be structurally different. They both are rule-based, composed of IF...THEN type units. Forward chaining systems may or may not have a specific goal.

In the forward chaining mode, the *premise* of each rule is sequentially examined. If information exists in working memory that allows the premise to be true, then the conclusion of the rule can be drawn and added to working memory.

As might be imagined, rules further down in the knowledge base may fire, adding information to working memory. This information may then allow for the firing of a rule further up in the knowledge base. Because this is the case, the procedure is an iterative one. The inference engine begins with the first rule and works its way down through the entire knowledge base, firing each rule for which the premise can be confirmed as true. After this first pass through the knowledge base, the system begins anew with the first rule. This process continues until either the goal is met, or until a pass through the knowledge base results in no new rules being able to fire.

The reader should be able to use the knowledge base in figure 3.1 to illustrate how a forward chaining inference system would use these knowledge chunks. *If* the system were first supplied with key values of expressions such as "product-category," "status-of-target-market," and "age-of-target-market," the system would begin with kb-2 and examine each rule's *premise* to see if the conclusion could be noted.

The system would continue to run through the knowledge base until either a value for "where-to-advertise" was found, or a complete pass through the knowledge base resulted in no rules firing. If the system were provided with the same information that the user supplied in Dialogs 1 and 2 of figure 3.2, the forward chaining system should arrive at the same conclusions for the value of "where-to-advertise." It would do it using a different inferencing technology, however.

Forward chaining systems have not been as popular in the first group of available development tools as have been backward chaining systems. Generally, to add value to backward chaining approaches, some tool vendors have also allowed the user the option of forward chaining. This means that the user can request that a knowledge base be processed in a forward or backward manner. The popularity of strictly backward chaining systems compared to forward chaining systems may result from the more intuitive nature of the former, and perhaps most importantly, the rather obvious nature of a wealth of backward chaining applications. In some sense, forward chaining applications may be more difficult for a new system designer to identify. This phenomenon may turn out to be a function of the market's sophistication, and could change as industry gains experience with the use of knowledge system development.

It should be noted that both forward and backward chaining systems often employ sophisticated algorithms to enhance the efficiency of the chaining process.

In addition, they may allow the user to control the processing of a knowledge base by exercising various inferencing options. The purpose of this discussion is to clarify some of the more fundamental aspects of what inferencing is, and how knowledge systems might be differentiated from traditional computer application development tools.

FRAME-BASED SYSTEMS

The rule-based systems described above offer a powerful scheme for representing knowledge. They provide a method of describing patterns among the values of parameters. For example, consider the following rule:

```
If multiple-purchase-lock-out = true
and inventory-use-correlation = true
then promotion-strategy = convenience-purchasing.
```

This rule describes a pattern in the values for multiple-purchase-lock-out and inventory-use-correlation. When this pattern is found, the rule concludes a new value for promotion-strategy. As such, rule-based knowledge systems allow the developer to describe meaningful patterns and conclusions based on those patterns. In the simple rule-based systems described above, these patterns are described in terms of *individual parameters* (such as "multiple-purchase-lock-out") and their *values* (such as "true").

An alternative to the simple rule-based systems described above is the frame-based approach. Frame-based systems expand upon the use of simple parameters and values to describe meaningful patterns. While there are many distinctions among the ways in which specific tools implement the concept of frames, in general, they all provide a richer method for describing the underlying concepts about which the rules will reason.

Using a frame-based tool, a developer might describe key underlying entities in the problem domain, and the relationships among them. For example, in the area of product promotion, one might hypothesize that an important, high-level concept is that of a *promotion device*. A promotion device might be a trial-size container, a coupon, a rebate, a free sample, etc.

In a frame-based system the developer could begin by specifying the *attributes* that the concept of a promotion device might have. These attributes might be things such as target markets, cost to the company, historical effectiveness, appropriate product categories, speed of market impact, effectiveness for new product introduction, etc. The entity "promotion device" could be defined as a frame with these attributes.

In addition to describing entities such as this, composed of many attributes, most frame-based systems allow the developer to create relationships among frames. For example, *coupons* are a kind of promotion device, and have some of the attributes of promotion devices in general. However, coupons also have some attributes of their own. These are not shared by other promotion devices. Examples of unique attributes might be the media for their distribution, the sub-types of coupons (i.e., cents-off or progressive purchase refunds), the size of the coupon, how it is redeemed, etc. Continuing in this way, the developer may define another entity, *cents-off coupons*, as a subcategory of coupons in general. Cents-off coupons will have some unique attributes, and some that are shared with the larger class of coupons, and the even larger class of promotion devices.

In this discussion, promotion devices, coupons, and cents-off coupons are general concepts. Frame-based systems allow the developer to describe multi-dimensional concepts such as these, and the relationships among them. In this case, there are clear hierarchical relationships, where promotion-devices are a superset of coupons, and cents-off coupons are a subset of the coupon concept. The hierarchical relationships among concepts such as these, the attributes that are general to all, and those which are specific to each level, can be represented in these structures known as frames.

The reader familiar with database management systems may see similarities between frames and tables. Each frame is like a table in that it describes a grouping of related information. In tables, column names define attributes of items in the table. These column names serve much the same purpose as do the attributes in frames. In a database, each row represents a record, or an individual entry. Similarly, in a frame-based system, each individual row or record is known as an instance of the frame. Each frame may have many instances.

Using the examples above, an application developer may describe the general concept of a cents-off coupon and its attributes as a frame. Rules may be added to help evaluate the effectiveness of various cents-off coupons that were issued in the past year on a market-by-market basis. These rules are written to refer to frames and their attributes.

Rule-based systems describe meaningful patterns and the conclusions to be drawn when these patterns are found. Frame-based systems enrich the ways in which the world is represented and increase the sophistication of the patterns that can be described.

All of the prototype systems described in this book, with DEALMAKER the only exception, were developed with simple rule-based tools. The DEALMAKER application was created with a frame-based system, in which frames have been developed for such entities as markets, retailers, manufacture's deal offers, and the like. Attributes of each of these entities have been defined. For example, manufacturer's deal offers have attributes such as performance requirements, case allowance, manufacturer, brand, the markets in which it is offered, etc.

Similarly, the frame describing retailers has attributes such as retailer name, markets, and the like. Rules in the DEALMAKER application refer to these entities, and have a form much like the example below:

IF there is an instance of a manufacturer' s deal offer, and it is offered in
some set of markets,
AND
there is an instance of a retailer that operates in one of these markets,
THEN
put the manufacturer' s deal offer on the list of deals under consideration by
the retailer.

This type of rule is written in very general terms, referring to frames and
attributes of frames. When the system is run, this type of rule will find all
manufacturer' s deal offers and put them on the lists of deals to be considered by
all retailers who operate in the relevant markets. The price for using frame-based
systems in an increased complexity in defining the entities that make up a
problem area. The benefit comes from being able to write more powerful rules
that reference these entities.

Frame-based systems are more difficult for developers who are unfamiliar
with AI techniques. The method of knowledge representation seems to be less
intuitive than the familiar structure of simple IF....THEN rules. However, in the
hands of experienced developers, frame-based systems offer a more robust
technology for creating larger and more complex applications.

Frames provide methods for defining entities, their attributes, and
interrelationships. As stated above, these objectives are very similar to those of
relational database management systems. This similarity of purpose has not gone
unrecognized by knowledge system tool developers. In many cases, users have
already modeled entities in their world as interrelated data tables. Their data
models are similar in purpose and structure to the frames they would create in a
knowledge system application.

Many tool providers are allowing the developer to easily move data stored in
database management systems into frame-based applications. That is, a
marketing information system may have data tables that define entities such as
past promotions. The column names that make up these tables might include type
of promotion, beginning date, ending date, brand, etc. Such a table might contain
many records representing individual past promotions.

In a knowledge system application, the developer might also represent past
promotions as a frame with similar or identical attributes. Moving data about
specific past promotions from the data management system into the knowledge
system would greatly enhance the reusability of the data. Sharing and reusing data
across applications is one of the primary reasons users employ data management
systems. Increasingly knowledge system tool developers are providing the
facilities necessary to allow this type of data sharing.

SUMMARY

There are many features and functions that distinguish commercially available knowledge systems. Most of these tools have the objective of being usable by developers unfamiliar with artificial intelligence programming techniques. In general, these tools allow the developer to represent knowledge as rules. Rule-based systems can be operated with either a backward- or forward-chaining approach to reasoning. These two approaches to reasoning are associated with different problem types.

Simple rule-based systems allow for patterns to be described as a series of parameters and their values. More sophisticated systems also provide the developer with frames. Frames provide a richer and more sophisticated technology for describing the entities the system will reason about. In general, simple rule-based systems with backward-chaining inference systems have proven easiest for novice developers to learn. There is a rich set of problems that are well-suited to this type of tool. Most of the systems described in this book have been developed with these relatively simple tools.

Larger and more complex applications seem to require more sophisticated tools. Frame-based systems provide a growth path for knowledge system developers interested in increased power.

NOTES

1. This chapter is based upon the material in chapter 2 of *Knowledge Systems for Business: Integrating Expert Systems & MIS*, John Gallagher, Prentice Hall, 1988.

CHAPTER 4

EXPERT SYSTEMS IN MARKETING:
AN INTRODUCTION

This chapter describes the implementation of a small marketing expert system in M.1 and in IBM' s Expert System Environment, thus making the reader familiar with an actual marketing system as well as the working of an expert system tool.

The tool is described in some depth because one of the tenets of our work is that the move of such tools from artificial intelligence laboratories into the commercial marketplace is providing the marketing systems' community with a new resource for supporting and enhancing marketing decision making. Hence, it is felt that familiarity with a typical tool enhances the ability of the reader to grasp and understand the role that expert systems can play in marketing.

THE PROMOTION ADVISOR KNOWLEDGE BASE

The objective of this knowledge base is to provide advice to a marketing manager regarding the promotion of a particular brand of a product. The ultimate outcome of a consultation with the promotion advisor is advice regarding which specific *promotion devices* the manager should employ. Promotion devices refer to methods such as coupons, in-pack premiums, rebates, contests, etc.

However, before specific promotion devices can be recommended, the system must identify appropriate *promotion strategies*. Product promotion strategies used in the knowledge bases are taken from the following set:

Trial. This strategy is used to provide incentives and mechanisms for consumers to be introduced to the product and its benefits.

Retrial. Under certain conditions, it is best for the consumer to experience use of the product more than one time, and a retrial strategy is appropriate.

Continuity.   Under other conditions, it is desirable to induce consumers to develop a repetitive pattern of purchasing the product. Continuity refers to continuity of purchase.

Convenience. Still other conditions will dictate a convenience purchase strategy. This approach induces the consumer to purchase substantial quantities of the product at one time.

Each of these promotion strategies is applicable under different conditions; however, conditions may overlap in such a way that more than one strategy may be appropriate at one time. In order to choose among the available strategies, the promotion advisor requests information about the following circumstances:

1. Characteristics of the brand item
2. Performance of the brand within the market and
3. Characteristics of the market

For example, a brand item such as toothpaste has different characteristics, in terms of product promotion, from potato chips. Also, a brand that is getting its share of the market and is widely known to consumers will be promoted differently from one that is a struggling new introduction. Finally, the market the brand is in has relevant characteristics. If it is a growing market, such as the market for soft drinks, one may promote a product differently than if the market is stable or declining.

The sample knowledge base, provided in the appendix of this chapter, is a small prototype intended for instructional purposes; however, it does reflect typical characteristics of prototype systems and provides a good point of departure for these discussions.

The prototype Promotion Advisor is intended to demonstrate ways in which a marketing problem might be structured and represented for a knowledge system application. Because of its prototype level of development, two aspects of system implementation will be discussed in the context of expert system development environments. First, the experience of developing the prototype will be described. Then, the prospects of expanding the system to a more complete, final form will be explored.

As the prototype Promotion Advisor currently exists, it is a stand-alone system with very few requirements for representing anything but rule-based knowledge. Also, there is little call for processing anything other than rules. If the system were to be expanded, however, these simple requirements would be placed under considerable stress. As the reader will discover, the prototype Promotion Advisor requests the end user to supply judgments regarding data. For example, the end user may be asked:

"Is the brand performing as expected with respect to market share?"

or,

"When compared to your competitors, is the percentage of your customers who are brand loyal high, medium, or low?"

In order to answer questions such as these, the end user must not only have access to relevant data, but must analyze it in an appropriate fashion, and then interpret it correctly. If the Promotion Advisor prototype were significantly expanded in power, it would be necessary for the system to access, analyze, and interpret these data. With this in mind, the prospects of expanding the prototype within each development environment will also be described.

EXAMPLE CONSULTATION

This section contains an example session with the Promotion Advisor in the M.1 expert system tool. This session provides an overview of the types of advice provided by the system, as well as the types of required information.

```
M.1> go

-------------------------------------------------
| Would you say that preference for this brand  |
| is overwhelming among those consumers who     |
| have tried it?                                |
-------------------------------------------------

       1.  yes
       2.  no
 >> 1 cf 80

-------------------------------------------------
| Would you say that market share is developing |
| normally for this brand?                      |
-------------------------------------------------

       1.  yes
       2.  no
 >> 2

-------------------------------------------------
| Would you say that the past 12-month trial rate |
| for this brand is high, medium, or low?         |
-------------------------------------------------

       1.  high
       2.  medium
       3.  low
 >> why
```

Your answer will help determine what
promotion strategy to use.

What is the rate of trial for this brand over
the past 12 months? In other words, of all
purchases of this brand, what proportion are
trial (rather than retrial or continuity)
purchases?

```
--------------------------------------------------
| Would you say that the past 12-month trial rate |
| for this brand is high, medium, or low?         |
--------------------------------------------------
```

```
    1.  high
    2.  medium
    3.  low
>> 3 cf 80
```

```
-------------------------------------------------
| Is this a brand with high consumer loyalty? |
-------------------------------------------------
```

```
    1.  yes
    2.  no
>> 1
```

```
-------------------------------------------------
| Would you describe the market for this brand |
|as growing, stable, or declining?            |
-------------------------------------------------
```

```
    1.  growing
    2.  stable
    3.  declining
>> 1
```

```
-------------------------------------------------
| Would you describe the numbers of consumers who |
| have used this brand in the past month as lower |
| than the number who used it over the past six   |
| months?                                         |
-------------------------------------------------
```

```
    1.  yes
    2.  no
>> 1 cf 80
```

```
-------------------------------------------------
| How would you compare the percent of your    |
| customers who are totally brand loyal versus |
| the percent for your competitors?           |
-------------------------------------------------
```

```
    1.  low
    2.  medium
    3.  high
>> 3
```

```
-----------------------------------------
| Is this product one for which multiple  |
| purchasing keeps consumers out of the   |
| market?                                  |
-----------------------------------------
```

```
    1.  yes
    2.  no
>> 1 cf 80
```

```
-----------------------------------------------
| Is this a brand for which consumer inventory  |
| is correlated with user consumption?          |
-----------------------------------------------
```

```
    1.  yes
    2.  no
>> 1
```

```
-----------------------------------------------
| Is it true that a consumer must use this      |
| brand several times in order to appreciate    |
| this brand's benefits?                        |
-----------------------------------------------
```

```
    1.  yes
    2.  no
>> 2
```

The strategies the system recommends are:

```
    sys_strat = trial (89%) because rule6 and rule4 and rule1.
    sys_strat = convenience (70%) because rule10 and rule9.
    sys_strat = retrial (40%) because rule7.
```

```
-----------------------------------
| Do you agree with this strategy? |
-----------------------------------
```

```
    1.  yes
    2.  no
>> 2
```

```
-----------------------------------------
| Select the strategy(ies) you prefer     |
| from the list below.  You may include   |
| certainty factors.                      |
-----------------------------------------
```

```
    1.  trial
    2.  retrial
    3.  continuity
    4.  convenience
>> 1 cf 90, 4 cf 60
```

```
    **  The system is now seeking marketing device.  **
```

```
device = own_brand_coupon (93%) because rule17 and rule14.
device = sampling (90%) because rule17 and rule14.
device = trial_size (90%) because rule17 and rule14.
device = pack_premiums (82%) because rule17 and rule14.
device = container_pack_premiums (81%) because rule17 and rule14.
device = bonus_pack (81%) because rule17 and rule14.
device = refund_coupons (76%) because rule17 and rule14.
device = free_mail_in_low_proof_premiums (72%) because rule17 and
       rule14.
device = high_value_single_unit_refunds (72%) because rule17 and
       rule14.
device = group_refunds (72%) because rule17 and rule14.
device = high_value_smaller_sizes_price_pack (72%) because rule17
       and rule14.
device = generic_refunds (70%) because rule17 and rule14.
device = feature_display_allowances (70%) because rule17 and
       rule14.
device = promotion_advertising (70%) because rule17 and rule14.
device = progressive_refunds (66%) because rule17 and rule14.
device = free_mail_in_premium_high_proof_required (60%) because
       rule17 and rule14.
device = contests (54%) because rule17 and rule14.
device = in_pack_games (54%) because rule17 and rule14.
device = high_value_multiple_unit_refunds (48%) because rule17
       and rule14.
device = off_invoice_allowances (43%) because rule17 and rule14.
device = continuity_catalog_premiums (36%) because rule17 and
       rule14.
device = cross_ruff_coupons (0%) because rule17 and rule14.
device = self_liquidating_premium (0%) because rule17 and rule14.
device = low_value_refunds (0%) because rule17 and rule14.
device = normal_low_value_price_pack (0%) because rule17 and
       rule14.
device = high_value_multiple_unit_price_pack (0%) because rule17
       and rule14.
device = sweepstakes (0%) because rule17 and rule14.
```

This system illustrates several important features of expert systems. which are implemented in expert system tools such as M.1. First, they allow for uncertainty, as shown in the response to the first question concerning the degree of consumer preference for the brand. In this example, the response provided was " 1 cf 80" indicating that the user of the system was 80 percent certain that the preference for this brand is overwhelming among those consumers who have tried it. This type of certainty in the state of the world can be combined with another type of certainty: certainty in the application of the system' s knowledge to a situation.

This second type of certainty is contained in some of the rules, as shown in the appendix. For instance, the first rule (rule1) states:

```
if ow = yes
then sys_strat = trial cf 50,
```

where ow refers to overwhelming preference and sys_stat refers to the promotion strategy the system will recommend. In English, this rule says: If there is overwhelming preference for the brand, then the system is 50% certain that the appropriate strategy is trial.

These two types of certainty, input certainty and knowledge certainty, will combine in this case to produce an overall certainty that trial is the appropriate strategy. The various certainties in the system have in fact resulted in the system being 89% certain that trail is the appropriate strategy, as shown at the top of page 42. Such certainty factor algebra is a built-in feature of the M.1 tool and does not require additional programming.

Another important feature of expert system tools is the ability to communicate with the user about why a question is being asked. Near the top of page 40, the system asks the user "Would you say that the past 12-month trial rate for this brand is high, medium, or low?" Instead of providing one of the indicated answers, the user typed "why" and received an explanation along with another statement of the questions.

A third feature of such tools is the automatic trace of the reasoning which led to recommendations. At the top of the page the system recommends promotion strategies, with statements like:

```
sys_strat = convenience (70%) because of rule10 and rule9.
```

The user can examine rules 10 and 9 to understand the logic that led to the 70% confidence in convenience as the appropriate strategy.

These features of expert system tools are not unique to M.1, a PC-based tool well suited for rapid prototyping. When developing such systems for use in a large corporation, it is important to consider additional factors, which may lead to mainframe based tools discussed in the next section. To gain an appreciation of the development of a marketing expert system that might serve a large company, it is important that the reader be aware of some of the features of an industrial strength tool.

IBM EXPERT SYSTEM ENVIRONMENT

The Expert System Environment (ESE) has a lineage that extends to the artificial intelligence research community of Stanford University. ESE was an internal IBM system developed at IBM's Palo Alto Scientific Center. At that time, the system was known as PRISM (PRototype Inferencing SysteM). The designers of ESE have maintained formal and informal contact with the artificial intelligence research and development community at neighboring Stanford University, among others. ESE's rule-oriented representation schemes reflect some of this heritage.

ESE is at its best when used by developers with mainframe system development experience. The support environment for developing and editing knowledge bases in ESE is very strong, and well designed for users new to knowledge system concepts. However, one of the real strengths of this package is its ability to interface with external programs and data. This will be described in detail below; however, it should be said that using this strength requires knowledge of the world outside of ESE. ESE is the first commercially available knowledge system development environment offered by IBM, and is the first to run under IBM' s mainframe operating systems, CMS and MVS.

ESE is well suited for large-scale development projects. It offers the ability to structure knowledge bases into blocks of rules called Focus Control Blocks, or FCBs. Within any FCB, it is possible to implement either forward or backward chaining inferencing. And, within either forward or backward inferencing modes, ESE offers the developer considerable control over how rules are processed.

As a system development tool, it includes special editors, one each for parameters, rules, focus control blocks, groups, and interface screens. A parameter is a measurable or estimable quantity such as market share or a concept such as action. A rule is a chunk of knowledge that relates parameters. For example: " if market share is declining then action = reduce budget." Focus control blocks provide a means to segment the knowledge base into subsets in which each subset refers to knowledge about a small aspect of the overall system. For instance, there could be a market share analysis FCB that would examine market share data and draw conclusions about the proper actions. FCBs are important conceptual units used by ESE to structure and control processing within a knowledge base. Each FCB consists of collections of rules and parameters, which are focused upon a particular area of the application. FCBs are arranged in a hierarchical pattern, with one FCB, the ROOT, located at the top of the hierarchical tree.

Each FCB' s activity, at a high level of abstraction, is determined by its control text. For example, control text for one of the FCBs in the Promotion Advisor is:

ASK User_to_Set_Strategy
DETERMINE User_Strategy
DETERMINE Device
DISPLAY Sys_Strategy
DISPLAY (Strategy, Device).

The key words, ASK, DETERMINE, and DISPLAY, tell the FCB to first ASK the user for some information, then to use back chaining to DETERMINE the values of some parameters, and finally, to DISPLAY some results. Other key words that can be used in the control language include

ACQUIRE—acquire external data
DISCOVER—forward chain for the values of some parameter(s)
ESTABLISH—give control to another FCB
PROCESS —put ESE data in an external file for processing by another program.

In this way, the control text is part of a Control Language that directs the activity of an FCB in a procedural fashion. It is possible to add some limited conditional statements, so that certain activities will only be carried out under specified conditions. Every time an FCB is established, its control text determines its sequence of activity.

In the context of the Promotion Advisor, an FCB could be constructed for knowledge relating the nature of the brand item to the appropriate promotion strategies. Similar FCBs could be constructed for knowledge relating information about the brand' s performance in a market, and the nature of the market itself, to promotion strategies. In ESE, these FCBs can be regarded as separate, smaller knowledge bases, each with control over processing within that FCB.

INFERENCING AND DEALING WITH UNCERTAINTY

Parameters in ESE are like variables in traditional programming languages that can take on values. An example of a parameter in the Promotion Advisor would be "strategy," "device," or "inventory_use_correlation." In ESE there are four ways that parameters can take on values:

1. As the consequence of a rule
2. From user input
3. From a default value
4. From the execution of some external function

When parameters are defined in the parameter editor, the ways in which the system is allowed to determine values for parameter, and the order in which these methods are to be applied are determined by the "sourcing sequence" for the parameter. That is, a rule might state:

```
If inventory_use_correlation = 'yes'
then there is .5 evidence that strategy = 'convenience.'
```

In this case, if the system were back chaining and trying to determine a value for strategy, this rule might be used. If "inventory_use_correlation" were not known to the system, then it would attempt to derive its value. In order to do this, the system would consult the sourcing sequence for the parameter. The sourcing sequence might be:

```
Rule Consequent
User Will Input From The Terminal.
```

In this case, there are only two methods provided for finding the parameter's value, and the system would try determining that value first from other rules, and if that failed, it would ask the user for a value. The concept of a sourcing sequence is very powerful in directing the action of the inference engine. In the process of inferencing, therefore, it is possible, when seeking a value for a parameter, to stop the back or forward chaining activity, and temporarily execute a procedural routine. However, this routine must be written outside of the ESE environment and linked to the system.

Inferencing itself is conducted in either a forward or backward chaining fashion. The developer is able to direct this activity through the control text of a FCB. The instruction, DETERMINE, invokes backward chaining. For example, the control text of an FCB in the Promotion Advisor includes the instruction:

```
DETERMINE f3_Device.
```

This directs the system to use back chaining to find a value for strategy in that FCB.

In ESE, the user can tell the inference engine how to choose among rules which could all conclude a value for the parameter being sought. In the Promotion Advisor knowledge base, there are several rules that conclude with "then strategy = ." ESE can be instructed to consider these rules in different sequences, depending upon how they are to be ordered. ESE can order the rules in the following ways:

By certainty factors. In this case, the rules that conclude a value for the sought after parameter with the highest certainty factors are considered first.

By unknown premises. Here, relevant rules are arranged in such a way that those with the smallest number of unknown values in the premises are considered first.

Most true premises first.

Out of focus last. This directs the inference engine to first consider rules in the present FCB, then to look at already-processed and in-process FCBs, and finally to FCBs that have not yet been accessed.

There are some other methods of control for rule processing in the back chaining mode but they require more in-depth explanations than are appropriate in this review.

If forward chaining is desired for the value of a parameter, the control text of an FCB would state:

```
DISCOVER parameter.
```

Just as in the back chaining approach to inferencing, there are extensive controls that can be applied when considering rules in a forward chaining mode. The same methods for arranging rules for consideration that are available in back chaining are available in forward chaining. These controls are very powerful extensions to knowledge system development. They allow the developer to modify not only the direction of the search process, but also to tune the process to gain greater efficiencies.

ESE provides mechanisms for reasoning with uncertainty through the concepts of *certainty factors* and unknown information. Certainty factors are one of the fundamental features of knowledge systems, in that they allow for reasoning to take place under fuzzy, or unclear conditions. That is, in the process of decision making it is often the case that some facts lead one to believe, with varying levels of certainty, that some other fact may be true. Likewise, the decision maker may only have some evidence that certain key components in a situation are present, but, by the nature of the circumstances, cannot be absolutely sure. Because reasoning involves chains of implications, and there may be uncertainties in both the premises and conclusions of rules, there must be some method for representing and combining certainties during the reasoning process. For example, refer to the following rules:

```
Rule 1:
IF A IS TRUE THEN C IS TRUE

Rule 2:
IF B IS TRUE THEN C IS TRUE.

Rule 3:
IF A IS TRUE THEN C IS TRUE CF 80.

Rule 4:
IF A IS TRUE AND B IS TRUE THEN C IS TRUE.

Rule 5:
IF A IS TRUE OR B IS TRUE THEN C IS TRUE.

Rule 6:
IF A IS TRUE AND B IS TRUE THEN C IS TRUE CF 80.
```

In the examples above, Rule 1 states that A implies C, and Rule 2 states that B implies C. In most rule-based systems such as ESE, confidence in an assertion is represented by a certainty factor (CF) on a scale from -100 to 100. On this scale, -100 indicates that there is absolute certainty that the assertion is NOT true. A certainty factor of $+100$ indicates that there is absolute certainty that the assertion IS true. A certainty factor of 0 indicates that there is no certainty one way or the other. Of course, values all along the scale are usable, however only in integer form. If a certainty factor is not provided in the conclusion to a rule, or in a user's input, it is assumed that the assertion is made with CF 100.

If it were believed that A is true with a certainty factor of 70, and that B is true with a certainty factor of 90, and system were to apply Rules 1 and 2 only, there are two independent sources of information regarding the truth of C. Because, there are two independent indicators that C is true, belief in this assertion is *strengthened*. The system will combine the certainties from the two rules in the following manner. Rule 1 will result in a belief that C is true with a certainty factor of 70, because that is the level of confidence in A.

When Rule 2 is applied, confidence in C will increase to a certainty factor of 97. Rule 2 *increases* the system's confidence in C. Because there is a certainty factor of 90 that B is true, the system's confidence can move 90% of the way from its previous level of confidence in C toward absolute certainty. Because there had been a confidence in C of 70, there is a distance of 30 between this position and absolute certainty. The new fact that B is true with CF 90 allows 90% of the distance to be traversed. This increases confidence that C is true by 27 points (.90 * 30) along the scale to a total of 97 (27 + 70). This is very different from the concept of joint probabilities, and should not be confused with that mathematics.

In Rule 3, the conclusion is that C is true with a certainty factor of 80. If *only* this rule were encountered, and the system had knowledge that A were true with a certainty factor of 30, then it would conclude that C was true with a certainty factor of only 24. In the simple condition of passing the confidence in the premise on to the confidence of the conclusion, the rules of combining probabilities are followed, and the two certainty factors are multiplied (0.30 X 0.80).

Rule 4 has a compound premise, requiring BOTH A AND B to be true in order to conclude for C. If the system believed that A were true with a certainty factor of 70, and that B were true with a certainty factor of 80, then, if it consulted this rule only, it would conclude that C is true with a certainty factor of 70. Since BOTH A and B are required, the lower of the two confidence factors is used in calculating the confidence in the conclusion. This is equivalent to passing on the weakest link in the chain because BOTH are required.

In Rule 5, however, the truth of EITHER A OR B will allow one to conclude for C. If only Rule 5 were considered, and the system believed that A were true with a certainty factor of 70 and that B were true with a certainty factor of 80, then it would conclude that C is true with a certainty factor of 80. Because the premise states that EITHER *A* OR *B* will provide evidence for *C*, then the strongest evidence is carried forward.

Finally, if only Rule 6 were encountered, and the system believed that *A* were true with a certainty factor of 70, and that *B* were true with a certainty factor of 80, then it would conclude that *C* is true with a certainty factor of 56. Because *A* AND *B* are both required, the system' s confidence in the premise of Rule 6 is only 70. This is passed on to the conclusion through the multiplication of .70 and the conclusion' s confidence factor of 80, to produce a final certainty factor of 54 for the truth of *C*.

The methods described above for combining certainty factors have their roots in early knowledge system research and development. They are examples of certainty factor algebra. There are many other possible variations. However, the methods described above are the only methods available for use in the ESE system. While they have proven in many cases to be robust and generally useful, there are circumstances in which the developer may wish to employ different certainty factor algebras. In the ESE system, no options regarding certainty factor calculations are available. Again, this simplifies development by reducing choice. And, the choices made by the developers of ESE fit most application areas well.

In dealing with uncertainty, ESE allows for two types of inferencing rules, those with an IF premise, and those with an FIF (Fuzzy IF) premise. The distinctions between them are in the way in which the certainty factor of the conclusion of a rule is affected by the certainty factor of the premise. In an IF form, the certainty factor of the premise has no impact on the certainty factor of the conclusion. For example, consider the following rule:

```
IF USE_CORRELATION = 'YES' THEN STRATEGY = 'CONVENIENCE'
```

If USE_CORRELATION were known to equal to ' YES' with a certainty factor of 80, or a certainty factor of 60, or a certainty factor of 90, it would make no difference. The conclusion that STRATEGY = ' CONVENIENCE' would still be made with a certainty factor of 100. However, if the rule were in the FIF form:

```
FIF USE_CORRELATION = 'YES' THEN STRATEGY = 'CONVENIENCE,'
```

the certainty factor of the premise would effect the certainty factor of the conclusion. That is, it is converted to a decimal number and multiplied by the certainty factor of the conclusion.

The Promotion Advisor in ESE

Because ESE is essentially screen oriented in its consulting mode, each question presented to the user appears on a separate screen. To reproduce a complete consultation with the Promotion Advisor would take a number of somewhat repetitious pages. What is reproduced in figure 4.1, therefore, is a screen taken from a consultation session with the Promotion Advisor in ESE. This screen format is used throughout the consultation.

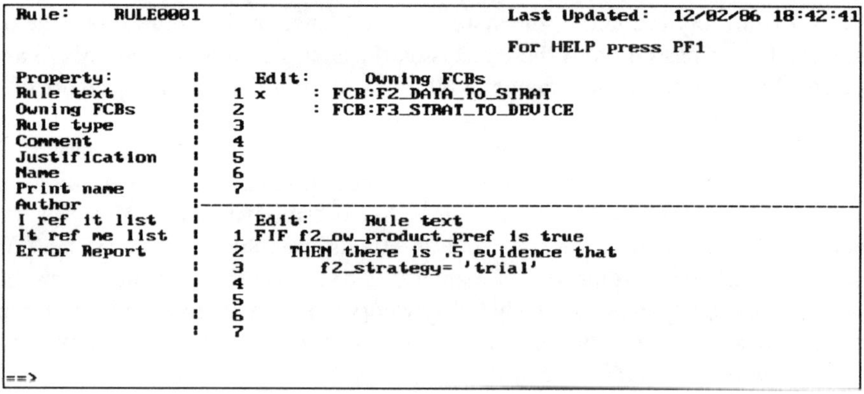

```
Rule:     RULE0001                          Last Updated:  12/02/86 18:42:41

                                           For HELP press PF1

Property:            I    Edit:      Owning FCBs
Rule text            I  1 x     : FCB:F2_DATA_TO_STRAT
Owning FCBs          I  2       : FCB:F3_STRAT_TO_DEVICE
Rule type            I  3
Comment              I  4
Justification        I  5
Name                 I  6
Print name           I  7
Author               I----------------------------------------------------------
I ref it list        I    Edit:      Rule text
It ref me list       I  1 FIF f2_ow_product_pref is true
Error Report         I  2     THEN there is .5 evidence that
                     I  3          f2_strategy= 'trial'
                     I  4
                     I  5
                     I  6
                     I  7

==>
```

Figure 4.1. Example of an ESE Screen

The screen is arranged so that the question appears in one area, with the possible responses displayed in a list below. In choosing among the possible answers, the user may simply place an x on the line in front of the appropriate answer. Or, they may place a number between zero and one (e.g., .80) on the line to indicate a certainty factor. With expressions that are declared as multivalued, the user may indicate more than one selection from the list. In the case of input that is not to be taken from a set of possible answers, the user may simply enter the character string or number the system needs.

To the right of the question-and-answer area are displayed the values of the program function, or PF keys. The PF keys can be used for single keystroke access to several options when a question is asked. For example, the user may request that the system discuss why the information is being sought, or what the system is asking for. That is, if the question is unclear, the developer may have provided a long prompt when creating the parameter, which would result in a second, often more detailed explanation of what is being asked.

For each of the major components of the system (i.e., rules, parameters, FCBs, etc.), there is a facility for the developer to add comments and notes. For example, when creating rules, the developer can add comments and justification text to the rule. When the documentation is printed, these types of information are printed along with the more common information, such as the text of the rule. The user has some control over just how verbose the printout will be, and what areas of the system will be documented.

The Promotion Advisor was implemented using the Root, and two additional FCBs. One of them is used to reason from the characteristics of the brands, performance of the brand in the market, and characteristics of the market to derive system recommendations for promotion strategies. The second FCB reasons from the strategies the user agrees to in order to arrive at final recommendations for specific promotion devices.

The interested reader can explore knowledged-based systems in more depth by reading *Knowledge Systems for Business*.[1] This book uses the Promotion Advisor as a springboard for discussing issues involved in building expert systems.

APPENDIX

PROMOTION ADVISOR KNOWLEDGE BASE IN M.1

kb-1: goal = device.

kb-2: initialdata = [sys_strat,strategy].

kb-3: legalvals(sys_strat) = [trial, retrial, convenience, continuity].

kb-4: multivalued(sys_strat).

kb-5: legalvals(strategy) = [trial, retrial, convenience, continuity].

kb-6: multivalued(strategy).

kb-7: multivalued(device).

rule1:
    if ow = yes
    then sys_strat = trial cf 50.

kb-8: question(ow) = [Would you say that preference for this brand is overwhelming among those consumers who have tried it?]

kb-9: legalvals(ow) = [yes,no].

kb-10: automaticmenu(ow).

kb-11: enumeratedanswers(ow).

kb-12: explanation(rule1) = [Your answer will help determine what promotion strategy to use based on blind taste tests (or the like) or based on purchase history, is it clear that consumers consistently prefer this brand to others in the category?]

rule2:
    if share = yes
    then sys_strat = retrial cf 50.

kb-13: question(share) = [Would you say that market share is developing normally for this brand?]

kb-14: legalvals(share) = [yes,no].

kb-15: automaticmenu(share).

kb-16: enumeratedanswers(share).

kb-17: explanation(rule2) = [Your answer will help determine what promotion strategy to use. Is this brand performing as expected with respect to market share?',nl]

```
rule3:
    if past_12 = medium
    then sys_strat = continuity cf 80.
```

kb-18: question(past_12) = [Would you say that the past 12-month trial rate for this brand is high, medium or low?]

kb-19: legalvals(past_12) = [high,medium,low]

kb-20: automaticmenu(past_12).

kb-21: enumeratedanswers(past_12).

kb-22: explanation(rule3) = [Your answer will help determine what promotion strategy to use. What is the rate of trial for this brand over the past 12 months? In other words, of all purchases of this brand, what proportion are trial (rather than retrial or continuity) purchases?]

```
rule4:
    if past_12 = low
    then sys_strat = trial cf 80.

rule5:
    if loyalty = low
    then sys_strat = convenience cf 50.
```

kb-23: question(loyalty) = [Is this a brand with high consumer loyalty?]

kb-24: legalvals(loyalty) = [yes,no].

kb-25: automaticmenu(loyalty).

kb-26: enumeratedanswers(loyalty).

kb-27: explanation(rule5) = [Your answer will help determine what promotion strategy to use. How strong is this brand's consumer franchise? Are people generally repeat purchasers or is there a lot of switching among brands in this category?]

```
rule6:
    if growth = growing
    then sys_strat = trial cf 50.
```

kb-28: question(growth) = [Would you describe the market for this brand as growing, stable or declining?]

kb-29: legalvals(growth) = [growing,stable,declining].

kb-30: automaticmenu(growth).

kb-31: enumeratedanswers(growth).

kb-32: explanation(rule6) = [Your answer will help determine what promotion strategy to use. How would you describe the growth rate for this',nl,'product category?]

rule7:
    if six_to_one = yes
    then sys_strat = retrial cf 50.

kb-33: question(six_to_one) = [Would you describe the numbers of consumers who have used this brand in the past month as lower than the number who used it over the past six months?]

kb-34: legalvals(six_to_one) = [yes,no]

kb-35: automaticmenu(six_to_one).

kb-36: enumeratedanswers(six_to_one).

kb-37: explanation(rule7) = [Your answer will help determine what promotion strategy to use. Is the number of consumers who have used this brand in the last month a lot lower than the number who have used it over the last six months?]

rule8:
    if share_of_con_p = low
    then sys_strat = continuity cf 50.

kb-38: question(share_of_con_p) = [How would you compare the percent of your customers who are totally brand loyal versus the percent for your competitors?]

kb-39: legalvals(share_of_con_p) = [low,medium,high].

kb-40: automaticmenu(share_of_con_p).

kb-41: enumeratedanswers(share_of_con_p).

kb-42: explanation(rule8) = [Your answer will help determine what promotion strategy to use. How would you compare the percent of our customers who are totally brand loyal versus the percent for our competitors?]

rule9:
    if lock_up = yes
    then sys_strat = convenience cf 50.

kb-43: question(lock_up) = [Is this product one for which multiple purchasing keeps consumers out of the market?]

kb-44: legalvals(lock_up) = [yes,no]

kb-45: automaticmenu(lock_up).

kb-46: enumeratedanswers(lock_up).

kb-47: explanation(rule9) = [Your answer will help determine what promotion strategy to use. If consumers load up on this product will it remove them from the market for a long enough time to give us a competitive edge? Can we preempt competitor's sales by loading up the consumer?]

```
rule10:
    if use_corr = yes
    then sys_strat = convenience cf 50.
```

kb-48: question(use_corr) = [Is this a brand for which consumer inventory is correlated with user consumption?]

kb-49: legalvals(use_corr) = [yes,no]

kb-50: automaticmenu(use_corr).

kb-51: enumeratedanswers(use_corr).

kb-52: explanation(rule10) = [Your answer will help determine what promotion strategy to use. Does the consumption rate for this product increase when consumers have a lot of it in their pantries? Will consumers use more if they have more on hand?]

```
rule11:
    if con_purch = yes
    then sys_strat = retrial cf 50.
```

kb-53: question(con_purch) = [Is it true that a consumer must use this brand several times in order to appreciate this brand's benefits?]

kb-54: legalvals(con_purch) = [yes,no].

kb-55: automaticmenu(con_purch).

kb-56: enumeratedanswers(con_purch).

kb-57: explanation(rule11) = [Your answer will help determine what promotion strategy to use. Is this a brand whose benefits aren't obvious after only one use? Does it take a consumer several trials before s/he can say s/he prefers this brand over another?]

```
rule12:
    if display(['The strategies the system recommends are:']) and
        do(show sys_strat) and
        user_agrees = yes and
        sys_strat = A
    then strategy = A.
```

kb-58: question(user_agrees) = [Do you agree with this strategy?]

kb-59: legalvals(user_agrees) = [yes,no]

kb-60: automaticmenu(user_agrees).

kb-61: enumeratedanswers(user_agrees).

kb-62: explanation(rule12) = [If you agree with this strategy the system will proceed directly to finding a suitable marketing device for your product. If you disagree you will be asked to select the strategy(ies) you prefer and the system will use your selections to find a device.]

```
rule13:
    if user_agrees = no and
       user_strat = B
    then strategy = B.
```

kb-63: question(user_strat) = [Select the strategy(ies) you prefer from the list below. You may include certainty factors.]

kb-64: legalvals(user_strat) = [trial, retrial, continuity, convenience]

kb-65: automaticmenu(user_strat).

kb-66: enumeratedanswers(user_strat).

kb-67: explanation(rule13) = [You may select one or more of the strategies listed. Then the system will proceed to find suitable marketing devices using your strategies. The strategies you select replace the strategies the system recommended.]

kb-68: when found(strategy) = display([The system is now seeking marketing device. **]).

```
rule14:
    if strategy = trial
    then device = sampling cf 100 and
         device = trial_size cf 100 and
         device = own_brand_coupon cf 100 and
         device = pack_premiums cf 80 and
         device = free_mail_in_low_proof_premiums cf 80 and
         device = high_value_single_unit_refunds cf 80 and
         device = group_refunds cf 80 and
         device = high_value_smaller_sizes_price_pack cf 80 and
         device = refund_coupons cf 60 and
         device = container_pack_premiums cf 60 and
         device = generic_refunds cf 60 and
         device = bonus_pack cf 60 and
         device = feature_display_allowances cf 60 and
         device = contests cf 60 and
         device = promotion_advertising cf 60 and
         device = in_pack_games cf 60 and
         device = progressive_refunds cf 40 and
         device = off_invoice_allowances cf 40 and
         device = cross_ruff_coupons cf 0 and
         device = free_mail_in_premium_high_proof_required cf 0 and
         device = self_liquidating_premium cf 0 and
         device = continuity_catalog_premiums cf 0 and
         device = high_value_multiple_unit_refunds cf 0 and
         device = low_value_refunds cf 0 and
         device = normal_low_value_price_pack cf 0 and
         device = high_value_multiple_unit_price_pack cf 0 and
         device = sweepstakes cf 0.

rule15:
    if strategy = retrial
    then device = sampling cf 80 and
         device = trial_size cf 100 and
         device = own_brand_coupon cf 100 and
         device = pack_premiums cf 80 and
```

```
            device = free_mail_in_low_proof_premiums cf 80 and
            device = high_value_single_unit_refunds cf 80 and
            device = group_refunds cf 80 and
            device = high_value_smaller_sizes_price_pack cf 80 and
            device = refund_coupons cf 60 and
            device = container_pack_premiums cf 60 and
            device = generic_refunds cf 20 and
            device = bonus_pack cf 60 and
            device = feature_display_allowances cf 60 and
            device = contests cf 60 and
            device = promotion_advertising cf 60 and
            device = in_pack_games cf 60 and
            device = progressive_refunds cf 20 and
            device = off_invoice_allowances cf 20 and
            device = cross_ruff_coupons cf 0 and
            device = free_mail_in_premium_high_proof_required cf 0 and
            device = self_liquidating_premium cf 0 and
            device = continuity_catalog_premiums cf 0 and
            device = high_value_multiple_unit_refunds cf 80 and
            device = low_value_refunds cf 0 and
            device = normal_low_value_price_pack cf 0 and
            device = high_value_multiple_unit_price_pack cf 0 and
            device = sweepstakes cf 0.

rule16:
    if strategy = continuity
    then device = sampling cf 0 and
            device = trial_size cf 0 and
            device = own_brand_coupon cf 60 and
            device = pack_premiums cf 60 and
            device = free_mail_in_low_proof_premiums cf 0 and
            device = high_value_single_unit_refunds cf 20 and
            device = group_refunds cf 20 and
            device = high_value_smaller_sizes_price_pack cf 80 and
            device = refund_coupons cf 100 and
            device = container_pack_premiums cf 100 and
            device = generic_refunds cf 60 and
            device = bonus_pack cf 80 and
            device = feature_display_allowances cf 60 and
            device = contests cf 0 and
            device = promotion_advertising cf 60 and
            device = in_pack_games cf 60 and
            device = progressive_refunds cf 60 and
            device = off_invoice_allowances cf 20 and
            device = cross_ruff_coupons cf 0 and
            device = free_mail_in_premium_high_proof_required cf 80 and
            device = self_liquidating_premium cf 0 and
            device = continuity_catalog_premiums cf 100 and
            device = high_value_multiple_unit_refunds cf 0 and
            device = low_value_refunds cf 20 and
            device = normal_low_value_price_pack cf 80 and
            device = high_value_multiple_unit_price_pack cf 60 and
            device = sweepstakes cf 0.

rule17:
    if strategy = convenience
    then device = sampling cf 0 and
            device = trial_size cf 0 and
```

```
device = own_brand_coupon cf 60 and
device = pack_premiums cf 60 and
device = free_mail_in_low_proof_premiums cf 0 and
device = high_value_single_unit_refunds cf 0 and
device = group_refunds cf 0 and
device = high_value_smaller_sizes_price_pack cf 0 and
device = refund_coupons cf 80 and
device = container_pack_premiums cf 100 and
device = generic_refunds cf 60 and
device = bonus_pack cf 100 and
device = feature_display_allowances cf 60 and
device = contests cf 0 and
device = promotion_advertising cf 60 and
device = in_pack_games cf 0 and
device = progressive_refunds cf 80 and
device = off_invoice_allowances cf 20 and
device = cross_ruff_coupons cf 0 and
device = free_mail_in_premium_high_proof_required cf 100 and
device = self_liquidating_premium cf 0 and
device = continuity_catalog_premiums cf 60 and
device = high_value_multiple_unit_refunds cf 80 and
device = low_value_refunds cf 0 and
device = normal_low_value_price_pack cf 0 and
device = high_value_multiple_unit_price_pack cf 0 and
device = sweepstakes cf 0.
```

NOTES

1. John P. Gallagher. *Knowledge Systems for Business: Integrating Expert Systems & MIS*, Prentice Hall, 1988.

CHAPTER 5

TEXTBOOK PROMOTION ADVISOR

SYSTEM PHILOSOPHY AND DEVELOPMENT

The last chapter provided an introduction to knowledge system by describing a small promotion expert system. This chapter discusses the development of a larger expert system, the Textbook Promotion Advisor, based upon promotion knowledge that is available in the public domain. This promotion advisor has the following characteristics:

It contains knowledge about promotions that is found in books and magazines.

It utilizes its knowledge to recommend a type of promotion device.

The advisor operates by asking the user a series of questions about a brand's situation in the market and the objective(s) of the promotion. The objectives are clustered into three main groups: consumer promotion, trade promotion, and advertising. Within consumer promotion there are objectives regarding consumer perceptions of a brand, brand usage, and competitive considerations. Trade promotion objectives are either inventory management or merchandising concerns.

After considering all of a user's objectives and brand circumstances, the advisor recommends a list of promotions. The consultation continues if couponing is on this list, for the user is offered the opportunity to have the system compile a list of appropriate coupon delivery vehicles.

What follows is a discussion of how the knowledge upon which the system is based is found, extracted, represented, and finally, how it is structured to accommodate the operation described above.

Knowledge Sourcing

First, we looked for those sources that might have advice on what promotional devices work in which situations. Our initial set of sources consisted of magazine articles in marketing publications like *Advertising Age* and *ADWEEK*, and chapters in books devoted to sales promotion management.

The magazine articles were located by 1) examining issues of the *Business Periodical Index* with the key word sales promotion in mind, 2) scanning past issues of the magazines in an effort to find special reports or editions devoted to consumer or trade promotion, and 3) perusing these same issues' regular columns to spot mentions of promotion that were missed or not noted in the *Business Periodical Index*. The marketing section of the business school library holds several how-to books on promotion, which discuss many of the more commonly implemented promotional tools like couponing, sampling, and sweepstakes.

Knowledge Extraction

Knowledge was extracted by first identifying knowledge chunks, and then filtering the words in these chunks to build simple rules. A knowledge chunk is a sentence or paragraph in which there is some relevant information or knowledge regarding the domain for which the knowledge base is built. For instance, a chunk of knowledge was identified by looking for words like *trial* or *in-pack premium* and tracing the authors' thoughts regarding these words.

The simplest rules unearthed were those that were phrased in the terms like: "<u>If</u> trial is what you want <u>then</u> saleable samples are what you need." The operative words in this knowledge chunk are the underlined ones: *if* and *then* because these are the words that introduce the promotion objective and the recommended device. The if-then structure also clearly defines the relationship between the two parameters.

There were also rules buried in chunks of knowledge that had to be constructed by paraphrasing the author's exact words. An example of this is seen in the following knowledge chunk quote:

> *For example, some detergent manufacturers have in-pack continuity programs that encourage the consumer to continue to purchase the brand time after time.*[1]

There are also rules that flow out of one long comment on the nature of promotional devices, which really contain more than one rule. In these instances, the knowledge engineer must disentangle several rules from a series of recommendations. An example of this follows:

An analysis of a number of successful trial-size programs has revealed that a brand in its introductory phase, during product restructuring, or during a new copy platform introduction can be an ideal candidate for a trial-size event.[2]

These examples of knowledge chunks represent most of those supporting our textbook promotion advisor. Whether the advice is buried in verbose language or presented in bullet form, we found that a systematic approach (via an if-then mentality) coupled with patience yields simpler representations of the knowledge.

Knowledge Representation

The knowledge representation form used in ESE is a rule-based one, consequently, we extracted if-then rules from the public domain knowledge chunks.

In order to extract if-then rules we had to approach the knowledge chunks with that structure in mind. In so doing, we became aware of the distinctions that needed to be made between possible if-premises or conditions. We had to make sure that in translating chunks to rules we retained the author's conditions for his/her promotion recommendation. To make this distinction clearer, look at the following two knowledge chunks:

The in-store premium (in-pack or near-pack) directed at children and indirectly at their mothers is extremely effective in moving a series of flavors in a line by creating continuity of purchase.[3]

Self-liquidating premiums can be quite effective in extending the advertising image.[4]

In analyzing the first chunk it seems that the author recommends the use of in-store premiums if the marketer wants items in one line to reinforce one another in a predominantly children food/beverage category. There are two conditions here so this must be reflected in the rule as well:

```
if goal = line-extension trial and
target market is children = yes
then promotion = in-pack premium
```

Similarly, if only one condition or situation is stated in a knowledge chunk, as in the second one above, then the premise of the rule need only have one clause as follows:

```
if goal = extend advertising image
then promotion = self-liquidating premium
```

There are only a few multiple-premise rules in the Textbook Promotion Advisor, because the recommendations were often based on only one conditional piece of information. So in this sense as well we can say that the resulting knowledge system is shallow.

The problem of knowledge extraction and representation is one of pattern-matching in which the expertise is captured mimicking the way an expert sees patterns by relating input and output. An experiential base allows the expert to build subtle links between situations and important factors when considering a problem such as a choice between competing alternatives. In so doing, the expert builds a list of necessary conditions that translates into multiple-premise rules in the knowledge engineering context.

In other words, as the expertise moves from shallow to deep, so too does the complexity of the knowledge representation. In the case of our Textbook Promotion Advisor, had the underlying knowledge been richer, our system would have had more multiple-premise rules.

Another element missing from our rules is the certainty factor. We could not find degrees of belief or certainty in the recommendations proposed by the various authors, nor did we feel it appropriate to impose our own certainty factors on the advice. For these two reasons, the rules in the Textbook Promotion Advisor are not labeled with measures of certainty.

We feel that the task of deciding the relative appropriateness of the recommendations is a subjective one, and thus a proprietary one. Each marketing organization has its own risk profile, and should therefore assign certainty to the advice itself, in the absence of public domain expertise.

Associated with the form of knowledge representation is the reasoning or inferencing strategy. Though ESE provides both forward and backward-chaining reasoning strategies, we utilized only the latter inferencing process. The reason for this is that a system designed to advise a marketer on promotion management in effect chooses between alternatives by weighing the pros and cons of a situation in a diagnostic manner. Backward-chaining is the better strategy for this kind of application.

Knowledge Structure

Initially the Textbook Promotion Advisor knowledge base had no structure because the knowledge chunks from which the rules were extracted, and the rules of the knowledge base themselves, were not grouped or classified in a structured manner. Any one knowledge source provided a few, varied promotional devices as tools to use in reaching a few, varied promotional objectives. None of the sources contained a structure for making decisions on promotion management.

The implication, for the user of an advisory system based on an unstructured knowledge base, is that the user is subject to a tedious, time-consuming, and to some extent, redundant or irrelevant interrogation every time s/he consults the system. Since a typical user of such an advisory system would be a novice to sales promotion, an introduction and encouragement of a structured thought process seemed necessary and thus provided the reason to attempt to impose a structure on the set of rules as well.

The fact that the knowledge system tool we used, ESE, provides a way to control a consultation, via the FCB knowledge format, allowed us to take advantage of this control structure. The FCB format contains control text which directs the system, and FCBs can be placed in a network in which they are linked to one another by the control text and by rules, thus allowing certain consultation paths to be established.

A structured thought process that is, to some degree, free of repetition and lengthy consultations, calls for a branched system in which there are several paths over which the questions that flow from the knowledge base can lead the user. The goal of this structuring process was thus to create a focusing system.

The first step in developing such a structure was to list values of the parameters contained in the extracted rules. Parameters can be viewed as facts about the domain. A primary parameter in our system, which is found in every rule, is PROMOTION. PROMOTION is the container of the many promotional devices, such as " in-pack premium" or " refund." The rest of the parameters refer to promotional objectives and take on values like " extend advertising image" or " fast trial." Rules relate the facts associated with parameters to one another, so in trying to group the rules, we had the option to either group by the objective parameters or by the promotional devices captured in the PROMOTION parameter. The latter criterion led to a system in which the user would have to know either something already about the promotional devices in order to choose which device(s) to look at further, or answer some preliminary questions that would narrow the scope of devices and thus focus the consultation. It seemed that grouping the rules based on the objectives' parameters would lay a better foundation for a structure that would lead the user back to the strategy, and even further back perhaps, to the situation that called for promotional activity. In other words, the user of a system based on an objective-structure would think about the objectives and the reasons behind them, so the focusing process would proceed according to what the user knew about the situation and not about the possible solutions.

We chose to group the rules according to the objectives. The first step in grouping the rules was to list all the objectives. This was an important step because we found that there were several objectives that were redundant in that the objectives outlined in the knowledge chunks were the same but they were phrased differently. An example of this is seen by comparing the lines below:

" increase long-term market sharey"

" long-term share increase"

It' s clear that the objective is the same in both of these lines, but if we had blindly coded the rules, we might have duplicated several. The point is that in listing the objectives, we had to decide on the unique phrasing of each objective.

The next step was to look across these objectives to see if there were some common denominators, or natural groupings. Grouping the objectives was the crucial step. Guided by marketing knowledge, we were able to distinguish, for example, between trade-oriented promotions and consumer-oriented promotions. Beyond this initial distinction we then found that there were objectives within trade promotion that were geared towards affecting retail inventories and several that dealt with merchandising issues. These distinctions formed several of the branches in the consultation network or tree.

The other branches were formed by considering, for example, how the groups of trade promotion objectives might be clustered. This aspect of the structuring process was not explicitly drawn from the list of objectives as was the facet described above. What we found was that we could make two clustering divisions.

First, we determined that promotional considerations for new and established brands are different. Second, we drew a line between promotional objectives that appeared to be shorter term in nature and those that were longer term considerations. The four branches that resulted from these two divisions constitute a controlling mechanism that guides a user down one of the four possible paths during a particular consultation. The process dictated by this structure is as follows:

The user decides whether his/her brand is new or established.

The user chooses to look at either short- or long-term promotional objectives.

The user is exposed to each of three groups of consumer promotion objectives with the following headings: Consumer Perception, Usage, Brand Situation. Within each group the user highlights those particular objectives of interest.

The user is exposed to two trade promotion groups: inventory management and merchandising. Again the user highlights the objectives of interest.

The user has the option of looking at a few advertising objectives and answering some questions which further clarify his/her promotional needs.

Promotional recommendations are made.

If couponing is suggested as one of the promotional devices, the user has the option of looking at those objectives s/he might consider in choosing a coupon delivery mechanism, like " on-pack" or " newspaper."

Coupon delivery vehicles are recommended.

Experience with this system was critical in the thinking of all the members of the Marketing Workbench Laboratory. Building the system served three goals:

1) It became a vehicle for learning to build expert systems in ESE.

2) It provided experience building a relatively large rule-based system.

3) It explored the degree to which public domain marketing knowledge supports the development of expert systems.

Outstanding results were obtained with all three goals. The most important one was the realization that in the promotion area the marketing literature would not carry one very far towards the development of an operational and useful expert system. There are many sources for such expertise, but each source tends to be very limited and not very rigorous; expert advice was offered without supporting evidence other than anecdotes and stories of successful promotions.

Even if one were to accept the public domain expertise as valid and reliable, a major problem still remains: The knowledge is very shallow and scattered. It was only after adding our own structure by clustering the objectives did the system begin to appear useful.

Does this mean that it is not wise to pursue the path of building knowledge systems from public domain knowledge? The answer depends upon whether the goal is a finished, or full knowledge system, full in the sense that all the necessary knowledge has been placed in the knowledge base. We came to consider the idea of partially filled knowledge bases that a company could take and complete by adding proprietary knowledge to the system.

The Textbook Promotion Advisor can be thought of as a partially filled knowledge base in the sense that it does not contain sufficient knowledge for the firm to rely upon it as an operational advisor. This incomplete state of the system is due to the incomplete nature of the public domain knowledge about promotion selection.

An incomplete or partially filled knowledge system does have considerable value because it provides several needed aspects of knowledge systems:

A method for representing the domain knowledge.

A method for structuring the knowledge so that it can be efficiently used in the reasoning processes.

A relatively complete knowledge base in terms of facts, models, and heuristics available in articles and books.

This knowledge base can be viewed as a starter kit that gets the final developer started on the process of building a system. As such, it provides both structure and substance. The finished system will thus contain knowledge from the public domain and the firm' s private knowledge bases.

Discussions with sponsoring firms indicated that the notion of partially filled systems has a lot of appeal. There seemed to be general agreement that each firm would want to customize any knowledge system to reflect its own knowledge; to " Kraftize" or " GFtize" the system.

No public domain sources of promotion knowledge are available that contain sufficient knowledge to go far beyond the knowledge base in the Textbook Promotion Advisor. Marketing research reports are available that provides a very rich source of marketing knowledge. As we were finishing the Textbook Promotion Advisor, a report that was full of pertinent knowledge was sent to us by one firm. For example,

You shouldn' t sell too much price pack at a time. Research shows that most extra business occurs in the first two weeks of retail distribution, so producing more than perhaps six weeks' supply of price pack is increasingly uneconomic.

Boldly flag your price reduction per product unit to consumers and the trade. We have conducted extensive in-store pricing audits of price packs and have found that trade mispricing can run as high as 20%.

Since these knowledge chunks purport to be based upon empirical research, they are much better knowledge sources than almost all of the ones found in the public domain, which provide little or no supporting evidence for the advice. And, the report contains knowledge that is not intuitively obvious, as is a significant part of the public domain knowledge.

Perusal of the marketing literature in other areas of the marketing mix (advertising, pricing, etc.) led to the same conclusion: Public domain knowledge in the marketing area is not a sufficiently rich source for building expert systems. This conclusion led us away from the idea of providing marketing advice via expert systems. While we continue to believe it is a viable use of expert system technology, we do not think that sufficient knowledge is available to university-based researchers to make the final system worth the effort.

Another insight was obtained while reaching these conclusions. A firm contains a number of marketing managers and marketing specialists, each applying expertise in the marketing area. Some of the expertise originated outside the firm in universities and research companies. Other expertise originated in the firm through experience and proprietary research. Since the building of expert systems requires the existence of expertise, university-based researchers can best build systems based upon knowledge that they have or to which they can gain easy access.

Experience in attempting to move the promotion advisor into one company indicates that outsiders have a very difficult time building expert systems based upon company knowledge. And it may be very difficult to accomplish the task from within the firm. One sponsoring company planned to fill up the Textbook Promotion Advisor using the knowledge of a very successful marketing manager in the firm. After examining the system, it was concluded that 100 hours of the expert's time would be required for the project. The manager's response, " I do not have three hours to devote to this task; 100 hours is out of the question."

All of these experiences point to the following process for developing expert systems in marketing: Focus on marketing areas that are very important, and areas where the knowledge is available from experts other than the marketing managers. Marketing managers are very busy and do not have sufficient time to devote to system development.

But where does such knowledge reside? With experts, obviously. These experts are in the universities, research firms, and in the marketing services departments in the firms. They are the media specialists, the promotion specialists, the marketing research professionals, etc.

As discussed in chapters 1 and 2, an area of great importance is the analysis of marketing data. And such analysis requires expertise. Peter Drucker[5] describes this situation quite nicely:

Information is data endowed with relevance and purpose. Converting data into information thus requires knowledge. And knowledge, by definition, is specialized.

Hence the decision was made to concentrate the laboratory's efforts on the eras of marketing systems. This decision received much more encouraging support from the sponsoring companies than did the efforts to computerize marketing knowledge. This is not surprising when one considers the fact that the systems were being designed for marketing managers and professionals. These people know marketing and like to practice it. They are not great analysts and do not enjoy the time-consuming effort involved in analyzing and understanding data. As one manager put it, " Any help on this front would be most welcome."

THE ROLE OF KNOWLEDGE AND INFORMATION

One of the issues that arise in the development of marketing systems is the need to integrate information and knowledge into one system. In the two promotion advisors, information is obtained by asking the user for the value of a parameter. A much more powerful system would acquire the required data from the firm's information system. *The Marketing Workbench* described an Information, Knowledge, Reasoning, Conclusion model which we will use to discuss the dual roles of information and knowledge in marketing systems.

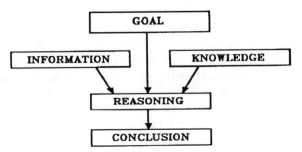

Figure 5.1. Information, Knowledge, Reasoning, Conclusion Model

Figure 5.1 presents a slightly expanded version of the model of how people process information. A person has a goal in mind, which causes him or her to acquire some knowledge that may be useful in reaching the goal. Using the media planning example from earlier in this chapter, a manager's goal may be to choose the type of advertising media. When the manager starts working on this goal, s/he would acquire the necessary knowledge by searching long-term memory, obtaining the necessary written material, or by consulting an expert. This knowledge could be: *use print if advertising liquor or cigarettes*.

At this point, the manager would be ready to start solving the goal by processing the requisite knowledge. This processing is termed *reasoning* in the model. As the manager reasons with the knowledge (*use print if advertising liquor or cigarettes*), s/he would recognize that information about the product category is important and thus must be obtained. After the appropriate knowledge and information have been obtained, a conclusion can be drawn.

Just as the manager would either know the product category or ask someone who did know, the expert system must do the same thing. Most of the early expert systems got their information by asking the user. MYCIN asked the user, the doctor, for information about the patient. Therefore a major component of the tool was the " screen toolkit" for developing customized input screens.

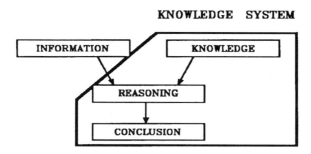

Figure 5.2. Knowledge System Model

Figure 5.2 illustrates how we can redraw this model to indicate the portions of the system that are part of the computer: goal, knowledge, reasoning, and conclusions. Information remains with the user.

In most marketing systems in place today, the marketing management information systems, reverse this model: Information is in the computer, and the other four components of the model remain with the user. The manager goes to the computer with a goal in mind, uses his own knowledge and reasoning processes to reach a conclusion based upon information obtained from the computer. This is illustrated in Figure 5.3.

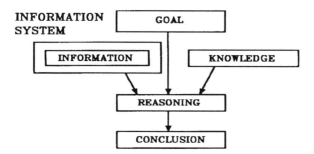

Figure 5.3. Information System Model

Neither of these two approaches seems to fit the needs of marketing systems, which have too many goals and too much data to permit managers to apply their own knowledge and reasoning processes. The situation calls for systems that contain all five of the components as illustrated in figure 5.4. In fact, most of the successful expert system tools have been evolving in this direction. The common approach is to expand the tool so that it contains hooks or connections to standard database systems. For instance, most vendors have or are working on a way to move data from a Structured Query Language (SQL) database into their tool when it is needed.

INFORMATION AND KNOWLEDGE SYSTEM

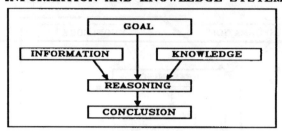

Figure 5.4. Information and Knowledge System Model

But, there is another characteristic of marketing systems that prevent these developments from being totally successful. Marketing information systems tend to contain raw data: unit sales and prices of an item in a geography during a time period. But the information required by the knowledge system usually involves a transformation of the raw data into parameters such as market share, percent change versus year ago, growth rate, brand development index, share of voice, and relative price. Values for these parameters are obtained by applying standard calculations to the data in the information systems. This is the main purpose of packages such as Express and Metaphor, packages that could be called marketing *information and analysis* systems.

The result is that knowledge systems in marketing need to go beyond the current practice of linking with database systems. They must link or couple with marketing information and analysis systems. This topic will be pursued in more depth in the next two chapters.

NOTES

1. Shultz, Don E., and Martin, Dennis G. "Sales Promotion —The Extra Step," *Strategic Advertising Campaigns*, Chicago, Crain Books, 1979, pp. 125-133.

2. Haugh, Louis J. "Promotion Trends: Trial Size Events Get Results," *Advertising Age*, October 11, 1982, p. M-53.

3. Meyer, Ed. "Do Your Sales Promos Lack Impact?" *Advertising Age*, October 6, 1980, p. 74.

4. Mahany, Gene. *Mahany on Sales Promotion*, Chicago, Crain Books, 1982.

5. Drucker, Peter. "The Coming of the New Organization," *Harvard Business Review*, January-February, 1988.

SECTION III:

APPLICATIONS

CHAPTER 6

A MARKETMETRICS KNOWLEDGE SYSTEM

THE PROBLEM

Marketmetrics refers to the modeling and statistical analysis of marketing data on the performance of brand items in markets over time. Marketmetrics is to marketing what econometrics is to economics. This chapter deals with the problem of estimating a marketmetrics model, such as a marketing response model or a forecasting model.

The traditional or conventional approach to this problem involves a trained analyst working with an interactive computer system. The analyst formulates a model, acquires the necessary data, uses an analysis package to estimate the parameters of the model and to produce associated statistics, examines the parameters and statistics to ascertain the appropriateness of the model, makes necessary changes in the model or estimation procedure, and reruns the analysis.

This iterative procedure can be put into the following series of steps: model formulation, model estimation, and model criticism. This procedure is repeated until an acceptable model is specified and estimated, or the process fails and the analyst concludes that the problem or the data are not amenable to this modeling approach.

This is a labor intensive activity that requires the services of an analyst who is highly educated or skilled in marketmetrics, the computer system, and the analysis package. The need for this type of talent has been minimal because of the lack of data to support the widespread development of " actionable" marketing models. When such models are needed, someone in the marketing research department is assigned this task. One firm reports that it takes at least one month to produce a good model for each and all brands in a category.

The situation is changing. As reported in *The Marketing Workbench*,[1] the microprocessor revolution is increasing the ability of the marketing research vendors to collect high-quality and timely data. These data will contain weekly data on brand-item sales at the store, chain, or market level, plus causal factors such as in-store promotions, newspaper advertising features, coupons, etc. Coupled with this data explosion is a transition from the concept of a national brand with one marketing program to the notion of regional (or local focus) marketing with many marketing programs.

These developments call for and permit the development of marketing models in a large number of markets. Consider the following typical situation. If the product category has 2000 items with data collected in 50 markets, then 100,000 models are possible. With chain level data and assuming 5 chains per market, the number of models increases to 500,000. If and when store level data are available and used in decision making, then it is possible to consider about 5 million models.

These numbers are based on the desirability of modeling at the lowest possible level. The statistical and managerial desirability of such modeling is the subject of additional study; this paper concentrates on methods for building a large number of models.

Hence, the traditional method of formulating, estimating, and criticizing a model is an area of appropriate study and research. This paper discusses a knowledge-based system for doing this type of analysis.

The major contributions are 1) the general concept, 2) architectures for coupling an expert system to a standard statistical package, 3) the representation of marketmetrics expertise via rules, and 4) the management of marketmetric models in a relational database management system.

MARKETMETRICS

The field of marketmetrics involves the application of statistical models and procedures to marketing problems and data. Applied marketmetrics involves cycling through the phases of model specification, model estimation, and model criticism.

One approach to improving the effectiveness or efficiency of this process involves the removal of the marketmetrician from the application of marketmetrics. This requires that we capture the theoretical and applied knowledge of the marketmetrician, and put this knowledge into the computer. The result would be a knowledge-based system that contains marketmetrics knowledge. We call this a Marketmetrics Knowledge System (M^2KS). This system requires two types of knowledge: marketmetrics theory and processes. We need to computerize both the theory of marketmetrics and the processes of applying that theory.

There are two types of marketmetric knowledge: theoretical and applied. Most of the literature concerns the theory, and the marketmetrician tends to pick up the applied knowledge via repeated application of the theoretical notions to real or academic problems. But, the literature does not contain much information to guide this application process.

The marketmetric and econometric literature contains adequate theory for model specification, estimation, and criticism. See for instance, Judge, et al.[2] But, the step-by-step processes one would go through in actually doing each of these activities tends to be missing from the literature. Naert and Leeflang[3] attempt to explore some of the process issues.

We use the term Generalized Modeling Procedure (GMP) to refer to the marriage of the theory and the process. The GMP is a process for applying the necessary marketmetrics theory to a specific problem. It is a statement of the model and data, and the processes one would use to estimate, critique, and refine the model.

The GMP refers to the procedure used to build an application model. Additionally, we can identify another type of process model that is useful in this work. Specifically, the theoretical aspects of marketmetrics can be decomposed into subject matter areas, and process models can be developed that show how the theory in that area can be applied.

For instance, the modeler may assume that the disturbances are not autocorrelated. The literature contains a number of methods for testing this assumption, along with statements about the conditions under which these tests are appropriate. These tests are part of the criticism aspect of the M^2KS.

Before the appropriate test can be brought to bear on a particular situation, the marketmetrician must identify 1) the tests, 2) the conditions that make each one appropriate, and 3) the process one would use in applying the various tests. The result could be termed a criticism procedure to indicate that it states a procedure for criticizing some aspect of an estimated model.

In the above example, the procedure for criticizing the autoregression assumption (of no autocorrelation in the disturbances) is to formulate an alternative assumption and to then utilize a standard statistic test to compare the data with the assumption and the alternative assumption.

In the typical case, the modeler would assume zero autocorrelation. To test this assumption, the criticism might involve the modeler making an alternative assumption of first-order autocorrelation. In this case, the Durbin-Watson test may be appropriate. But, three things can go wrong. First, the model could contain a lagged dependent variable, in which case the Durbin-h-test is appropriate. Second, the data may contain missing values, which would invalidate the usual method for calculating the Durbin-Watson statistic. Third, the Durbin-Watson test may lead to inconclusive results. In this case, there are several alternatives available, but additional information is needed to select the most appropriate test. The M^2KS would need to know how to detect and deal with such problems.

The construction of the M^2KS requires that process models be built for each area of criticism and that these process models be converted into a language that can be processed by the knowledge system. Further, the analysis package must be capable of producing the statistics that are needed by the knowledge system as it executes the various criticisms.

We can see from these descriptions that the development of the M^2KS involves two marketmetric activities: 1) capturing the theoretical aspects of marketmetrics and 2) capturing those aspects of marketmetrics that are unique to producing a particular marketing model. Both are essential to the system.

APPROACH

The approach discussed in this paper involves capturing the knowledge of a marketmetrician and putting it into a computer system so that the system can direct the analysis.

We assume that the application of marketmetrics involves several types of knowledge:

General marketmetrics knowledge about formulating, estimating, criticizing, and interpreting a marketing model,

Specific marketmetrics knowledge about specific problem domains, e.g., advertising models, coupon redemption models, and competitive structure models,

General marketing knowledge about marketing variables and their interrelationships,

Specific marketing knowledge about specific problem domains (e.g., advertising).

The general knowledge in the M^2KS will be available when needed to solve problems that are general to any and all modeling efforts. For instance, when dealing with time-oriented data it is necessary to detect and model autocorrelation in the model's disturbance term. The M^2KS should contain an autocorrelation detection module that can be used when needed.

Specific knowledge is called upon when dealing with a particular problem. For instance, in modeling advertising effects, it is necessary to know the allowable advertising lag structures and to be able to select the structure that matches the data and the product category being modeled. This knowledge may have to be blended with general marketing knowledge or with specific knowledge about advertising effects. For instance, it has been shown that brands that use image advertising will have a longer lag structure than those that use factual advertising.[4]

These different types of knowledge will be captured in a computer system that is designed to use knowledge, rather than the typical system that focuses on information. These knowledge systems are sometimes called expert systems, but we use the term *knowledge system* in recognition that our systems incorporate knowledge from many sources, not just a single expert.

COUPLED SYSTEM AS A HERMENEUTIC CIRCLE

Hermeneutics is a Greek word that refers to the study of methodologies of interpretation. We are adapting the term to describe the way we process information, knowledge, and reasoning by the interaction of two computer programs to solve marketing problems. Hermeneutics will refer here to the question-and-answer type of interaction between two programs that produces an increasing refinement of the solution to the problem at hand.

The term *hermeneutic circle* describes this interaction of two computers where the first computer formulates and asks a question and the second computer returns an answer. The first computer interprets the answer and refines its original question, and then asks a reformulated question. This circular processing is repeated until the questioning computer halts it, by using some predetermined criterion of correctness. The hermeneutic circle is not simply the movement from one state to another and then back again to the original state, but a progression of more and more refined questions with correspondingly refined answers, which continues until the questioner is satisfied. In this regard, it is somewhat similar to the cobweb model for reaching market equilibrium.

In the world of man and machine there has so far been a division of labor in the hermeneutic circle: The human expert formulates the questions, asks them, interprets the answers and then adjusts the questions while the computer receives the questions and returns responses. The human expert initiates and halts the entire process.

With the advent of expert systems, some of the human's expertise may be computerized as well. The human expert can begin to back out of the loop and two computer systems can be coupled together in the hermeneutic fashion described above. The human expert can use the computerized expert system as a tool to expedite and simplify his work. In turn, the knowledge system has software tools of its own to help it perform its task.

Expert systems tend to be good at reasoning, interpretation, and reformulation but not very good at handling statistical, numerical analysis, such as running regressions on autocorrelated time series data. A statistical package like Statistical Analysis System (SAS) is very good at numbers but not at reasoning about its own output. An expert system could be created that contains its own routines for doing statistical analysis, but at considerable cost. Such an expert system would be unnecessarily large and unwieldy; the statistical package would be specialized and hard to modify.

Our project takes advantage of the inherent strengths of the two systems and combines them by coupling the two. The human expert's thought processes and rules of thumb are embodied in the expert system, while the heavy-duty number-crunching is left to the more traditional statistical program. Coupling allows the expert system to call for the answers it needs from the statistical package as it proceeds through its reasoning and refining process.

The next section describes a simple application, which serves to illustrate such a dialogue between two systems. In this example, a human acts as the eyes and ears of each system.

A KNOWLEDGE-BASED ADVISOR

To understand the issues involved in building a marketmetrics knowledge system, it is informative to examine a simple system that advises a manager about the construction of a model. This example serves to 1) illustrate the use of rule-based systems to represent marketmetrics knowledge and 2) introduce the issues involved in coupling a knowledge-based system to a statistical system.

Knowledge-based systems are usually developed using an expert system shell that contains one or more methods for representing knowledge and methods for reasoning with that knowledge. One of the most widespread knowledge representation schemes is an IF-THEN rule. Systems that use this method are termed *rule-based systems*. A common method for processing the rules is a backward-chaining inference engine. See Harmon and King[5] for an introduction to these topics and Buchanan and Shortliffe[6] for a detailed discussion.

A knowledge-based system could be developed that advises a manager on the development of a marketing model. For exposition purposes, consider a simple time trend model of the form:

```
UNITS = A + B*TIME.
```

Given time-series data on units, such a model could be used to estimate the historical time trend and to produce forecasts. This is a very simple model, but one that serves to illustrate some of the issues in building a marketmetrics knowledge system.

Assume that the manager has the data in an analysis package, knows the mechanics of using the package, and requires assistance in applying the appropriate statistical procedures and tests. An expert marketmetrician has examined the model and the general class of data the manager will be using. This examination revealed two potential problems: non-linear trend and autocorrelation in the disturbances.

This marketmetrician decided that the manager should first check the linearity assumption because nonlinearity can show up as autocorrelation in the residuals and thus mask other sources of autocorrelation. After detecting and correcting for nonlinearity, autocorrelation can be examined. If present, autocorrelation can be corrected via an autoregressive disturbance process. This process was further developed into the following Generalized Modeling Procedure.

1. CHECK LINEAR ASSUMPTION

    A. FORMULATE A NONLINEAR MODEL:
       UNITS = A + B*TIME + C*TIME^2 + E
    B. USE ORDINARY LEAST SQUARES (OLS) TO ESTIMATE THE UNKNOWN PARAMETERS
    C. TEST THE STATISTICAL SIGNIFICANCE OF THE PARAMETER "C"
    D. DROP THE TIME^2 TERM IF INSIGNIFICANT AND REESTIMATE USING OLS; ELSE
       PROCEED

2. CHECK FOR AUTOCORRELATION

    A. OBTAIN DURBIN-WATSON STATISTIC FROM RESULTS OF STEP 1
    B. USE DURBIN-WATSON STATISTIC TO TEST FOR FIRST-ORDER AUTOCORRELATION
    C. IF DURBIN-WATSON TEST IS NOT SIGNIFICANT, THEN <u>FINISHED</u>

3. CHECK FOR HIGHER-ORDER AUTOCORRELATION

    A. MODEL THE ERRORS AS AN AUTOREGRESSIVE PROCESS OF ORDER N
    B. INITIALLY, SET N = 2
    C. USE YULE-WALKER EQUATIONS TO ESTIMATE THE MODEL
    D. USE T-TEST PROCEDURE TO TEST THE SIGNIFICANCE OF LAG COEFFICIENTS
    E. IF SIGNIFICANT, INCREASE THE LENGTH OF THE AUTOREGRESSIVE PROCESS AND
       REPEAT TEST
    F. CONTINUE UNTIL AN INSIGNIFICANT COEFFICIENT IS LOCATED
    G. REESTIMATE WITH CORRECT LAG LENGTH

This process was programmed in M.1, an expert system shell that uses a backward-chaining inference engine. The philosophy underlying this system is that the manager will interact with two programs: The analysis package for estimating and testing the model and the M.1 program which advises the manager on the application of the Generalized Modeling Procedure.

The following is the M.1 program that implements the Generalized Modeling Procedure:

```
goal = model.

kb-1:
if display('Run a model with a linear and a nonlinear term') and
```

```
    trend = ok and
    autocorrelation = ok
then model = correctly_specified.
```

kb-2:
```
if non_linear_term = insignificant and
   display('Drop the nonlinear term and rerun the model')
then trend = ok.
```

kb-3:
```
if non_linear_term = significant and
   display('Keep nonlinear term in the model')
then trend = ok.
```

kb-4:
```
if t_stat = T and (T< -1.96 or T>1.96)
then non_linear_term = significant.
```

kb-5:
```
question(t_stat) =
'What is the value of the t-statistics of the nonlinear term?'.
```

kb-6:
```
if t_stat = T and T> -1.96 and T<1.96
then non_linear_term = insignificant.
```

kb-7:
```
if durbin_watson_test = ok
then autocorrelation = ok.
```

kb-8:
```
if durbin_watson_statistic = D and
   D>1.5 and D<2.5
then durbin_watson_test = ok.
```

kb-9:
```
if durbin_watson_statistic = D and
   (D<= 1.5 or D>= 2.5) and
   display('Re-estimate the model using the AR1 option')
then autocorrelation = ok.
```

kb-10:
```
question(durbin_watson_statistic) =
'What is the value of the Durbin-Watson statistic?'
```

The goal statement (goal = model) initiates the backward-chaining process, which causes the M.1 inference engine to seek a value for the parameter model. It does this task by searching the rule base for a rule that concludes a value for model, i.e., which has the term " model=" as the THEN part of the rule. Since the first rule (designated kb-2 for knowledge base entry #2) meets this condition, M.1 will process it next. This processing causes M.1 to try to process the clauses in the premise of the rule. The first such clause instructs the user to run a model with linear and nonlinear terms. Then the second clause causes M.1 to seek a value for the parameter trend. It does this by searching for a rule that concludes a value for trend; this lead M.1 to the kb-3.

> M.1 continues in this manner until it can either successfully find a value for the parameter model, or it fails.

If this knowledge-based system were operating by itself, it would need to ask the user for values of the *t*-statistics and the Durbin-Watson statistic. The result would be a dialogue with the user which calls for the user to input two numerical values. The system' s instructions to the user are shown in <u>underlined</u> type in the following panel:

```
M.1> go

Run a model with a linear and a nonlinear term

What is the value of the t-statistics of the nonlinear term?
>> 1.33

Drop the nonlinear term and rerun the model

What is the value of the Durbin-Watson statistic?
>> 1.42

Reestimate the model using the AR1 option

model = correctly_specified (100%) because kb-3.
```

This backward-chaining inferencing procedure can be illustrated using an M.1 feature that produces a trace of its operation as it processes the rules. A portion of this trace is discussed below.

M.1 is started with a goal statement, in this case it is " goal = model." This causes M.1 to seek a value of model, and it does so by examining the rules one at a time until it finds one that concludes a value for model. That is, it looks for a rule that ends with a statement of the form: " then model = ." It finds such a rule in kb-2, as shown in the following portion of the trace:

```
Seeking model.
Invoking kb-2:
  if display('Run a model with a linear and a nonlinear term')
  and trend = ok and
  autocorrelation = ok
  then model = correctly_specified.
```

M.1 has invoked this rule, which means that it will start to process each premise until it finds one that is not true. It starts with the first premise, which tells it to display a string of material on the screen. It does so, which produces the following statement on the screen:

```
Run a model with a linear and a nonlinear term.
```

M.1 has satisfied the first premise by simply following its command to display the string. Then it turns its attention to the second premise in the rule (trend = ok), which causes it to seek a value for the trend parameter. It does this just as it sought a value for model: It looks through the rulebase until it finds a rule that can conclude a value for trend. This search is successful at kb-3, which causes M.1 to invoke this rule.

```
Seeking trend.
Invoking kb-3:
  if non_linear_term = insignificant and
  display(Drop the nonlinear term and rerun the model)
  then trend = ok.
```

In invoking this rule, M.1 finds that it must determine a value for non_linear_term and it does so by looking for a rule that can conclude a value for non_linear_term. It finds such a rule in kb-5. These steps are shown in the next panel.

```
Seeking non_linear_term.
Invoking kb-5:
  if t_stat = T and (T< -1.96 or T>1.96)
  then non_linear_term = significant.
```

The same process is repeated one more time, causing M.1 to search for a rule that concludes a value for t_stat. But this time, it cannot find such a rule because the knowledge base does not know how to determine the *t*-statistic of the nonlinear term in the model. Since M.1 cannot find a rule to give it a value for t_stat, it knows that it must ask the user for a value. It searches the rulebase for a statement that will tell it how to ask the user for this value. As shown below, it finds this statement in kb-6 in the form of a question.

```
Seeking t_stat.
Using kb-6:
  question(t_stat) =
  'What is the value of the t-statistics of the nonlinear term?'
```

When M.1 processes kb-6, it displays the following on the screen, as instructed by kb-6:

```
What is the value of the t-statistics of the nonlinear term?
```

The user must then type in the value, which s/he obtains by looking at the regression printout where the value of 1.33 is obtained and typed at the prompt.

At this point, M.1 notes the value by placing it in its working memory, and it recognizes that it has found a value for t_stat:

```
Noting t_stat = 1.33 cf 100 because you said so.
Found t_stat.
```

Having satisfied kb-6, M.1 then returns to the rulebase entry, which has caused it to invoke kb-6; it returns to kb-5 and continues to process it in its attempt to conclude a value for non_linear_term. In so doing, it finds that the rule has failed because the value of t_stat (1.33) is neither less than −1.96 nor greater than 1.96. Since kb-5 will not provide the needed value for non_linear_term, M.1 looks for another rule that could provide such a value; it finds that kb-7 meets this condition. Its processing of this rule is shown below.

```
kb-5 failed.
Invoking kb-7:
   if t_stat = T and T> -1.96 and T<1.96
   then non_linear_term = insignificant.
```

Since it has already found a value for t_stat, it can go ahead and process this rule. The premises succeed, which allows M.1 to accept the rule and thus conclude a value for non_linear_term.

```
Already sought t_stat.
Noting non_linear_term = insignificant cf 100 because kb-7.
kb-7 succeeded.
Found non_linear_term.
```

Since it has found a value for non_linear_term, it can now return to the rulebase entry, which has caused it to seek the value in the first place. Hence, it returns to kb-3, where it finds that the first part of the premise is true. Then it processes the second part of the premise, which causes it to send the following message to the user.

```
Drop the nonlinear term and rerun the model
```

M.1 now notes that it has found the value of trend, which causes it to return to the rule that had directed it to seek a value for trend in the first place. This takes it to kb-2, where it sees that it must now seek a value for autocorrelation. These steps are shown below.

```
Noting trend = ok cf 100 because kb-
3.
kb-3 succeeded.
Found trend.
Seeking autocorrelation.
```

The process starts over again in the sense that M.1 starts looking for a rule that will conclude a value for autocorrelation, and it finds it in kb-8.

```
Invoking kb-8:
  if durbin_watson_test = ok
  then autocorrelation = ok.
```

This rule sends it down another trail in search of a value for durbin_watson_statistic.

These steps are repeated until M.1 recognizes that it must ask the user for a value of the Durbin-Watson statistic. Its rules lead it to put the following message on the screen:

```
Reestimate the model using the AR1 option
```

The user enters a value of 1.42 and M.1 continues to process its rules until it can conclude a value for model, which was the original goal. It does so, and draws the following conclusion:

```
model = correctly_specified (100%) because kb-2.
```

To use this two-program system, the manager would need to interact with both the statistical package and the knowledge-based system. Note that in this example, the manager simply does what s/he is instructed to do by the knowledge-based system. The manager reads the instructions on the screen of the knowledge-based system, types the appropriate commands on the keyboard of the analysis package, reads the appropriate statistic on the screen of the analysis package, and types this statistic on the keyboard of the knowledge-based system.

COUPLED SYSTEMS

The manager plays a unique role in the above example: s/he provides the interface between the two packages. The manager is sort of a *gossip* in the sense that s/he operates by listening to one package and telling another package what was said by the first one. This gossip function serves to couple the two systems, resulting in an application that is termed a *coupled system*. This new area of artificial intelligence involves the coupling of a numerical processing program with a symbolic or knowledge-based program. A recent volume of papers published on this topic presents a number of applications in engineering and scientific computing, which were discussed at a workshop.[7] The lead article[8] in that volume makes the following observation about the increased interest in coupled systems:

Two major reasons for the recent interest in coupling numerical and symbolic computing emerged during the workshop. The first is a need to assist those using complex numerical algorithms and programs. In order to solve many problems in business, science, and engineering both insight and processing are often needed. In many instances, insight into the problem-solving process must be gained in order to obtain a solution. In others, insight is needed to interpret computed results. And in still others, users need guidance and counsel in order to utilize the tools at their disposal. Historically, however, traditional computing has provided the user a great deal of accuracy, but none of these insights. Until recently, users have been left, for the most part, to their own devices when determining how to apply computing to the task at hand or interpreting the results of numerical programs. Coupled systems promise to integrate the explanation and problem-solving capabilities of expert systems with the precision of traditional numerical computing. A second major reason for coupling symbolic and numerical techniques is a need for computing tools of increasing power and usefulness capable of transcending the limitations of our traditional environments.

These reasons for going to coupled systems are very valid in marketing, particularly in the area of marketing analysis. The typical marketing manager is very capable of performing fundamental types of analyses and in interpreting the results. But, the more advanced analyses usually require the use of models, and most managers are not qualified and comfortable in dealing with models and modeling concepts. The following remarks by Little[9] amplify this point:

Managers do not like terminals. They are impatient and busy. They do not formulate problems in model terms because that is not the way they actually think. They want to think about strategy, not analysis. They will propose actions to be analyzed, but they will not do it themselves.

Given that models are required to answer some of the more interesting marketing questions, coupled systems seem to offer a useful approach to the implementation of marketing analyses.

THE MODELBASE

The M^2KS was designed to build a model of each of the items in a product category. Since a category may have hundreds or thousands of items, the output of the M^2KS would be the same number of models. For instance, the Italian sauce category contains about 2000 items. The application of the M^2KS to this category would result in 2000 models.

The traditional man/machine approach to this situation would result in a large stack of computer printouts. Just as there are too many items to be modeled by conventional methods, there will be too many models to analyze and understand by conventional methods. Just as M^2KS contains knowledge for building models, other systems could be built for analyzing, interpreting, and applying these models. This need for model access introduces the requirement to store the models in a machine-readable form.

Some work has been done in the area of representing models in a form which is usable by computer programs. Lennard[10] has discussed the notion of representing models as data in a database. We applied the same idea but deviated from Lennard's approach, which involved the use of a logical structure suggested by the principles of structured modeling.[11] The result is a modelbase.

After the coupled system builds a model, the results of the analysis need to be stored for convenient access at a later time. The statistical results are one of two types: model specific or coefficient specific. Model parameters such as R^2 have one value per model while parameters such as the t-statistic have values for each variable in a model.

EXAMPLE APPLICATION

Our initial coupled system implementation serves to estimate a marketmetrics model of a single brand item. As stated in the introduction section, a product manager has the opportunity to analyze every brand item in every market using scanner data that is readily available from data vendors. These databases contain weekly information on unit and dollar sales, price, retail newspaper advertisements, and in-store displays. Wittink, et al.[12] and Blattberg and Wisniewski[13] have demonstrated the viability of using existing marketmetric models and methods to estimate models of these items. Given the existence of these developments, the next step is to demonstrate the feasibility of using a knowledge-based system for such model estimation and analysis.

Wittink pools time-series and cross-section at the store level to estimate a multiplicative model, and Blattberg and Wisniewski aggregate store level data to the chain level to estimate a similar multiplicative model. Our experience with scanner data has shown that the marketmetric issues are similar in linear and multiplicative models. Therefore, we have elected to use a linear model to demonstrate the use of coupled knowledge and information systems.

This model is of the following form:

$$\text{UNITS} = B_0 + B_1*\text{PRICECUT} + B_2*\text{DISPLAY} + B_3*\text{FEATURE} + E$$

```
UNITS = weekly retail sales in units
PRICECUT = regular price - shelf price
DISPLAY = level of in-store displays
FEATURE = retail ad features in newspapers
         (column inches)
E = random disturbance term.
```

Although this is a very simple model, it is used here to illustrate the principles and operation of coupled systems. The data for this model are scanner data for the light-duty detergent category.

When estimating and evaluating this type of model, the marketmetrician goes through a series of steps involving data retrieval, preliminary data analysis, initial model estimation, model criticism, and model refinement.

GENERALIZED MODELING PROCEDURE

The following is the Generalized Model Procedure (GMP) used in this example.

Data Retrieval. M^2KS extracts data from SQL/DS for a particular brand item. The SAS/SQL-DS software produces a SAS dataset containing week, units, regular price, shelf price, display, and ad features.

Data Check. The system checks to see that the dataset exists, has sufficient observations, contains no holes (missing data), and has sufficient variation in each of the causal factors.

Initial Model Construction. Based upon the initial data check, the system formulates a linear model, as shown above, which contains the causal factors that pass the data check for sufficient observations and sufficient variation.

Initial Model Estimation. Ordinary Least Squares is used to estimate the initial model.

Autocorrelation Detection. One of the problems with time-series data is autocorrelation or serial correlation in the disturbance term (E). M^2KS detects first-order autocorrelation through the Durbin-Watson test.

Autocorrelation Correction. The system uses SAS's PROC AUTOREG to estimate the model if autocorrelation has been detected. The Yule-Walker equations are utilized to estimate the equation. An iterative procedure is used to arrive at the length of the disturbance lag structure. This procedure starts with a first-order assumption and increases the length until an insignificant autoregressive parameter is detected.

Model Storage. The final model is stored in two tables in SQL-DS via the SAS/SQL-DS software.

These various steps account for the currently implemented Generalized Modeling Procedure. Clearly, other aspects of marketmetrics could be implemented, such as tests and procedures for multicollinearity, heteroscedasticity, and lagged variables.

The next chapter explains the system's architecture and goes through a detailed description of the application of this Generalized Modeling Procedure.

DISCUSSION

Marketmetrics, which refers to the use of statistical analysis to model market data, is becoming important due to the increasing quality and quantity of market data. This data explosion has two implications:

1. Marketing managers will quickly grasp the need for models that provide an understanding of the factors which have been driving the business.

2. The demand for the models will outstrip the firm's ability to build them using conventional methods.

The second point is due to the limited talent and time to formulate, estimate, and refine the multitude of required models. One answer to this situation is the use of expert or knowledge systems.

A Marketmetrics Knowledge System is a knowledge-based system that directs the building of marketmetrics models. The system will contain the knowledge of one or more marketmetricians. Since this knowledge is not static, the system cannot be static. As the marketmetrician learns more about analysis and modeling, the M^2KS must be modified to contain this new knowledge.

This evolving nature of the M^2KS leads to the need for a symbiosis between the marketmetrician and the M^2KS. The marketmetrician will perform the following activities:

Develop models.
Develop Generalized Modeling Procedures.
Build the knowledge base or work with programmers who do the actual coding.

Monitor and audit the M^2KS.
Modify the M^2KS as new knowledge is acquired.
Handle difficult cases passed by the M^2KS.

This close working relationship between the marketmetrician and the M^2KS points to the need for both the human and the knowledge-based system to interact with the same analysis package. Hence the need for coupling a standard analysis package to a knowledge-based system. This need has resulted in considerable attention to the Application Program Interface and the various nuances of computer systems. Advances in facilities for such program-to-program communication will improve the performance of coupled systems. To introduce the reader to some of these issues, this chapter has included detailed discussions of architectures for building Marketmetrics Knowledge Systems.

The M^2KS can operate as a background task in the sense that it can function without an operator. Whenever a product category needs to be modeled, the M^2KS can be passed the name of the database containing the data and it will build the models and place them in the modelbase. These models are then available for later use.

Small example systems were used to illustrate the concepts of a marketmetrics knowledge system. A complete system would need to be much more sophisticated in the sense that it would need to be able to deal with all of the marketmetric issues that might arise in building a model.

For instance, our example systems only dealt with nonlinearity and autocorrelation. A more complete system would have to recognize the problem areas of autocorrelation, multicollinearity, heteroscedasticity, and residual diagnostics. In that case, rules such as the following would be incorporated in the system.

```
IF autocorrelation of the residuals is ok
            multicollinearity in the RHS-variables is ok
            heteroscedasticity in the residuals is ok
            diagnostics of the observations is ok
THEN the model passes the statistical tests
```

This rule could be the controlling rule, which drives the system to determine values for each of the four areas of concern. To succeed, the system would need additional rules for each area. For instance, the autocorrelation area could contain the rule:

```
IF DW_stat is ok
            Runs-test is ok
THEN autocorrelation of the residuals is ok
```

And, the diagnostics area could drive the system to look at a wide array of problem areas, as shown in the following rule:

```
IF Chow test is ok
            Ramsey test is ok
            Brown-Durbin-Evans test is ok
            Harvey-Collier test is ok
            Hausman test is ok
            Plosser-Schwert-White test is ok
            Godfrey-Wickens test is ok
            Rainbow test is ok
THEN Diagnostics is ok
```

The first clause of the premise instructs the system to determine if the Chow test is OK. Since the Chow test must be done in the statistical package, a rule like the following could cause the system to direct its search to the SAS system:

```
IF SAS PROC Chow reports insignificant results
THEN Chow test is ok
```

These are the types of rules one would need to capture and computerize the full set of marketmetric knowledge available to the trained marketmetrician.

Such model building is only one aspect of the ongoing process of model management. This process can be thought of as model building, model tracking, and model modification. Th M^2KS discussed in this paper would perform the first task: model building. Another system would be needed to track the models, i.e., to determine if they are performing correctly. When it was determined that a model was not performing correctly, yet another system might be used to modify the model in light of new data and evidence. All of these activities are candidates for knowledge-based systems.

The M^2KS is an example of a broader class of applications, which involves a knowledge-based system directing an analysis package in some analysis or modeling task. Although the M^2KS involves the coupling of the Expert System Environment with SAS, the concept is general enough to apply to almost any type of analysis package and any expert system environment.

A popular marketing decision support package is Express, which is used to view and analyze marketing data. A common activity with such a package is problem detection and analysis in which a manager spots a problem and then uses the system to find the possible causes of the problem. The following is a scenario of such an analysis, which was offered by Express's manufacturer, Management Decision Systems.

The problem: In a few regions, brand sales are down from last year or from the general trend.

POSSIBLE CAUSES	DATA TO LOOK AT
The whole category is down in those regions.	*Check category changes in all regions.*
There's new competition in test market.	*Search competitive data for new brands or sizes. If you discover any, then check 1) if the loss of share is proportionate to the brand's share level, 2) if there is a difference in prices, and 3) if there is a change in trade support.*
There's been a change in promotional or advertising strategy (your's or the competition).	*Check share of weighted value, using syndicated sources such as ACB or Majers for data about trade promotional strategy; check internal data to investigate your advertising changes.*
Your product's price (relative to the competition's) has changed.	*Using SAMI and/or Nielsen data, compare your price with theirs over time within one region. Use a scatter plot of relative price or price difference to look for a relationship with share.*
Distribution is down because the outlet has specific problems (strikes, weather, etc.), or an aggressive competitor is taking over distribution.	*Look at net distribution data (probably Nielsen, NRTI, or SARDI) to see whether distribution is down in those regions. If so, look at maximum distribution and out-of-stock to determine if the problem is in inventory or de-listing.[14]*

This is a type of problem known to the AI field as a *diagnostics* or *selection* problem. It occurs when something is broken and there are a number of possible causes. The system diagnoses the problem by selecting one or more of the causes.

A knowledge-based system would contain rules about the causes, their symptoms, and the measures one would make to detect each symptom. The resulting rule-based system backward-chains by hypothesizing a possible cause and trying to confirm the existence of the symptoms. It can be programmed to either stop after finding a possible cause that cannot be rejected, or to continue to examine all the known causes.

Our experiences with the M^2KS lead us to the conclusion that the easy part of this type of application is the development of the knowledge base. That is, it is relatively easy to arrive at a scenario or procedure such as the one shown above. And, representing this procedure as rules is also relatively easy. Also, there are other knowledge representation methods available such as frames and deamons, which enhance our ability to represent such knowledge. The hard part, given present technology, is the coupling of the resulting knowledge system to the analysis package.

This recognition leads to the recommendation that developers of marketing information, analysis, and decision-support systems should allow for their systems being driven by another computer program. They should begin to consider the notion that the user of their program may actually be another program, rather than a human.

Another finding from this research is the desirability of storing the results of one analysis for use in subsequent analyses. The modelbase, which stores the results of the modeling activity, can be generalized to store and make available the results of other analyses, such as the findings of the analysis depicted above which finds the reason for declining sales. If the results of this analysis are stored every time the analysis is run, then other systems can search for patterns in the analyses and thus reach higher-level conclusions. This is a form of meta-analysis currently practiced by academic researchers. Meta-analysis can become a part of managerial analysis given a method for storing and accessing the results of each managerial analysis.

There are a number of research questions involved in modeling the new marketing data:

What are the appropriate models for understanding the competitive and market mix effects in a local store or chain?

Under what conditions are the different models optimal?

What is the best estimation technique for each model?

Can we develop a Generalized Modeling Procedure that contains answers to these types of questions and can be used to guide a modeler?

Can we program a computer to advise the modeler on the application of the Generalized Modeling Procedure to a specific store, chain, or market?

Given a model of a brand in a store, how do we communicate its marketing implications to a typical marketing manager?

Can we train a computer to do such communication?

Can we teach a computer to analyze and model marketing data, determine the marketing implications of the analyses and models, select the appropriate marketing mix to deal with the situation, and write a marketing plan that discusses the analysis and models, explains their implications, and presents the marketing plan in English language?

This latter question is the mother of all of the others and can be considered the ultimate research question.

NOTES

1. McCann, John. *The Marketing Workbench*, Homewood, IL: Dow Jones-Irwin, 1986.

2. Judge, George G., W.E. Griffiths, R. Carter Hill, Helmut Lutkepohl, and Tsoung-Caho Lee. *The Theory and Practice of Econometrics*, Second Edition, New York: John Wiley & Sons, 1985.

3. Naert, Phillippe, and Peter Leeflang. *Building Implementable Marketing Models*, Netherlands: Martinus Nijhoff, 1978.

4. McCann, John M., and E. Ojdana, Jr. "On the Form and Length of the Advertising Distributed Lag Structure," *Marketing in the 80' s*, R. Bagozzi (Ed.), American Marketing Association, August, 1980.

5. Harmon, Paul, and David King. *Expert Systems: Artificial Intelligence in Business*, New York: John Wiley & Sons, 1985.

6. Buchanan, Bruce G., and Edward H. Shortliffe. *Rule-Based Expert Systems*, Reading: Addison-Wesley, 1984.

7. Kowalik, Janus S. *Coupling Symbolic and Numerical Computing in Expert Systems*, Amsterdam: North-Holland, 1986.

8. Kitzmiller, C. T., and J. S. Kowalik. "Symbolic and Numerical Computing in Knowledge-based Systems," in Kowalik, Janus S., *Coupling Symbolic and Numerical Computing in Expert Systems*, Amsterdam: North-Holland, pp. 3-17, 1986.

9. Little, John D. C. "Decision Support Systems for Marketing Managers," *Journal of Marketing*, Vol. 43, Summer, p. 22, 1979.

10. Lennard, Melanie L. "Representing Models as Data", *Journal of Management Information Systems*, Vol II, No. 4, Spring, pp. 36-48, 1986.

11. Geoffrion, Arthur M. "An Introduction to Structured Modeling," *Management Science*, 33(May), pp. 547-588, 1987.

12. Wittink, Dick R., Michael J. Addona, William J. Hawkes, and John C. Porter. "SCAN*PRO: A Model to Measure Short-Term Effects of Promotional Activities on Brand Sales, Based on Store-Level Scanner Data," Working Paper, 1987.

13. Blattberg, Robert C., and Kenneth J. Wisniewski. "Price-Induced Patterns of Competition," Working Paper, Graduate School of Business, University of Chicago, 1986.

14. Management Decision Systems, Inc. "How to Use Your Express Marketing Decision Support System," 1983.

CHAPTER 7

THE COUPLED SYSTEM

This chapter discusses the architecture for coupling knowledge systems to traditional management information systems that produced the Marketmetrics Knowledge System. This chapter is intended for the technical reader interested in the implementation of the coupled system. Whereas chapter 6 discussed what the system does, this chapter focuses on how it does it.

ARCHITECTURE CONSIDERATIONS

It is recognized that computer packages that are good at doing the actual statistical analysis may not be the best for implementing the knowledge system. Expert system tools or shells are emerging as devices for capturing knowledge and reasoning with the knowledge. These tools contain an inference engine, which uses one or more reasoning mechanisms to apply the knowledge to a particular problem. If these reasoning mechanisms are found to be appropriate to the problem at hand, then these packages can greatly facilitate the development of a knowledge-based system.

One drawback of using an existing package (rather than a high-level language such as Pascal or Lisp) to implement the knowledge system is the need to interface or connect the knowledge system to the analysis package. This interface requires a connecting mechanism for allowing one package to communicate with another. This set of diverse packages calls for an overall architecture that specifies the components, their roles, and their interconnections.

The Marketmetrics Knowledge System (M^2KS) is a system for applying marketmetrics knowledge in a way that a good marketmetrician would apply the same knowledge. Just as the marketmetrician interacts with an analysis package, the marketmetrics knowledge component of the M^2KS interacts with an analysis package.

The M^2KS is composed of five entities: the database management system, the analysis software, the knowledge-based system, the user, and an interface through which the analysis and knowledge-based systems communicate. This is a modular approach in which the components are constructed from packages and languages that best suit the needs of that aspect of the problem. Languages for estimating a sales response function may be very different from languages that are suited to criticizing the resulting model.

The M^{2}KS includes a separate statistics/analysis package and a knowledge-based system. These two communicate with each other through other programs or facilities of the operating system. The M^{2}KS has been implemented using two different architectures. The initial hardware/software implementation of this broad concept was via the IBM 3270 AT and its High Level Language Application Program Interface (HLLAPI). This system provides the ability to run multiple mainframe sessions and multiple workstation sessions from the workstation, i.e., from the 3270 AT (see McCann[1] for a discussion of this computer workstation). In this system, each application program runs in its own presentation space.

In this original architecture, the HLLAPI interface module served one primary function: gossip. It was a gossip in the sense that it transferred what it heard from one presentation space to another presentation space. As a gossip, the interface module recognized that one component needed information from another component. It simply transferred the request from the requesting component to the providing component.

For instance, consider the situation in which the knowledge-based system is beginning to build a model. It needs to know the brand and account the user wants to analyze. It poses the appropriate command, which is received and interpreted by the gossip component of the interface module. This module captures the command and displays it on the user's display screen. It then waits for an answer from the user, captures this answer, and transfers it to the knowledge-based system. In this example, the knowledge-based system is the requesting component and the user is the providing component.

After receiving this information, the statistical analysis package would then retrieve the appropriate data and tell the gossip component that it was ready for the next command. The gossip would then send a message to the expert system that the statistical analysis package was ready. The expert system would formulate the next statistical analysis package command and pass it back to gossip, which would send it to the statistics package. This process would continue until a suitable model was built.

This initial implementation allowed us to prove the feasibility of this approach and to gain experience with the concept of a coupled system. However, it was a relatively clumsy approach because the two mainframe sessions had to communicate via a PC-based program. The resulting uploading and downloading of data was less than optimal.

SYSTEM CONSIDERATIONS

The 3270 AT and HLLAPI implementation used the gossip program as a means of coupling the knowledge system with the statistical system. An obvious question arises: Why not couple one system directly to the other one? That is, why not have the knowledge system communicate directly with the statistical system?

Our investigation into this question revealed that it is relatively easy to perform such program-to-program communication when the two programs are written in high-level languages such as Fortran and Lisp. Such an application has been reported in the plasma physics area.[2]

To take advantage of an existing analysis package and to use an expert system shell to increase programming productivity, one must couple existing packages. Consider the use of the Statistical Analysis System (SAS) instead of Fortran and the Expert System Environment (ESE) rather than Lisp. These packages were designed to communicate with the terminal screen, printers, and storage media; not to communicate with another package. We accomplished communication between ESE and SAS by using the file and message-handling capabilities of an IBM VM/CMS operating system, and not by modifying either ESE or SAS themselves.

Our experience with the initial implementation pointed to the desirability of running all the programs on the same system so that communications could take place more rapidly than over communications lines. Therefore, we built our prototype in one computer: an IBM 4381 running the VM/CMS operating system.

OVERVIEW OF THE FLOW OF CONTROL

The figure below illustrates the system's flow of control.

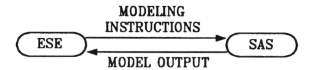

Figure 7.1. Flow of Control

The expert system initiates processing since it is in charge of reasoning about information and deciding what to do with it. It formulates the data needed for the statistical machine to run; these data may include generating code that the statistical machine can use or inserting parameters into prewritten sections of code or templates that the statistical machine will execute.

The expert system passes information in the form of data to the statistical package in the same way that a human user would pass the information. The statistical package cannot distinguish between a human user and the expert system machine since both the human and the expert system provide data and commands in the same fashion. Once the expert system has directed the statistical machine to start up, it suspends its own activity until the statistical package is finished with its assigned task. Processing by the statistical package is initiated by the expert system. It finds all the data and direction that it needs to finish its task. Once it is finished it returns control to the expert system.

The expert system can examine the results that were generated by the statistical package by looking at the output the statistical package generates. With this output, it reasons further about the problem and may direct the statistical package to do further analysis if necessary. The cycle finally halts when the expert system meets a predefined goal or criterion of correctness.

The SAS component of the system contains several prewritten SAS programs, or templates, which perform different tasks. (See figure 7.2.)

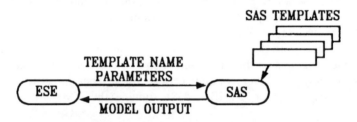

Figure 7.2. The SAS Component

For instance, there is a template for performing SAS' s AUTOREG procedure. This template requires two parameters: the model and the length of the autoregression disturbance model. The expert system tells the statistical system which of its templates to use; it also passes the parameters that the statistical system needs to complete the template before running it.

Key points to keep in mind when considering this coupled system are:

1. The expert system specializes in reasoning and controls the statistical system which specializes in number-crunching. The expert system poses the questions and reasons about the answers, which are supplied by the statistical system.

2. The knowledge system and the statistical analysis system use standard software packages: the ESE expert system and the SAS statistical software. Neither software package was modified in order to get them to work together.

3. The expert system and the statistical system need to interact, but both require some help since they are not built to communicate with each

other. Additional software and the resources of the operating system are used for communication between SAS and ESE. (See figure 7.3.) The expert system uses the assistance of a set of Pascal language external routines, and the statistical system uses the assistance of a controlling program written in REXX.[3]

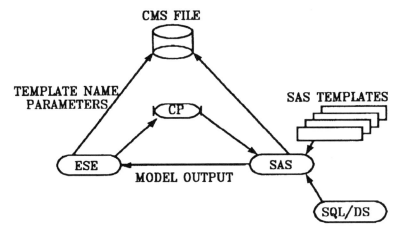

Figure 7.3. ESE-to-SAS Communication

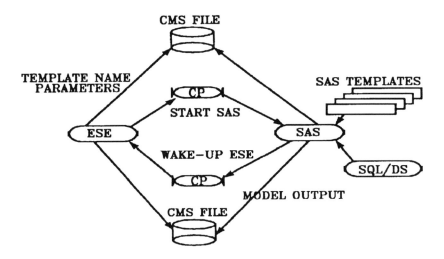

Figure 7.4. Coupled System Components

Both systems are running in the VM/CMS environment and take advantage of the CMS operating system' s file handling facilities. They can pass information back and forth using CMS files, but they also use the message handling utility in the operating system' s Control Program (CP).

ESE reaches SAS by going through Pascal, CMS, CP and REXX. CMS and CP provide file and message-handling capabilities, while Pascal routines and a REXX program front-ends ESE and SAS.

To complete the system, SAS must send its output back to ESE. The process is a mirror image of the ESE-to-SAS communication. SAS sends its output to a CMS file and sends a message to ESE via CP, which returns control to ESE. (See figure 7.4.)

These software components of the prototype are described in more detail in the following section.

COUPLED SYSTEM: OUTLINE OF COMPONENTS

The coupled system contains four major components: an expert system, a statistical analysis system, a database system, and their common operating system.

The Expert System

1. Expert System Environment (ESE)

ESE is IBM' s mainframe rule-based expert system shell. The knowledge base in ESE acts as the manager or controller of the hermeneutic circle. It formulates the questions to ask and directs the statistical system to retrieve information and calculate answers. It then reasons with the answers and asks further questions until it has solved the problem at hand.

2. Pascal External Routines

ESE needs a way to communicate with the outside world. A set of external routines are used to give ESE a link to the CMS operating system to allow ESE to

 a. Read an external (CMS) file
 b. Write an external (CMS) file
 c. Execute a CMS command
 d. Invoke CP to send a message to another machine
 e. Wait for a return message from another machine

The external routines allow ESE to manage data in a common area: the CMS file system. Once data is in a CMS file, it is accessible to other machines in the VM system. ESE can also import data generated by another machine via the CMS file system. In this way ESE is translating from its own data representation scheme (its knowledge base) to another (CMS disk files) that another machine can access. The external routines also allow ESE access to the control program (CP) message system, so ESE can send a message to another machine. It is in this way that the expert system part of the M^2KS gives directions and requests for information to the statistical system.

The Statistical Analysis System

1. Statistical Analysis System (SAS)

SAS allows the construction and execution of sophisticated models for data analysis. The SAS system, while not an expert system, has considerable knowledge about the description and analysis of numerical data. This knowledge is embodied in the SAS system' s set of callable subroutines, or PROCS.

SAS also has the ability to import a file into a program and use that file' s contents as part of the program code. The M^2KS takes advantage of this ability. The knowledge system generates code in a form that SAS can use. It tells SAS to import the code into one of SAS' s PROCS, or predefined templates.

2. REXX

Instead of sending messages directly to SAS, the knowledge system sends messages to an intermediary control program, which is running in the VM machine that also runs SAS. The control program is written in IBM' s REXX exec language. The REXX program we have written does the following:

a. Invokes SAS programs
b. Tells CP to send a message to another machine
c. Issues CMS commands for file management
d. Parses output files generated by SAS programs

When the knowledge system wants answers from SAS, it sends its request to the REXX exec program and lets that program take care of housekeeping, file management, running SAS programs, parsing SAS' s output files, and sending back confirmation messages that all tasks are complete. REXX is a suitable implementation language for the machine running SAS.

The Database System

Structured Query Language (SQL) is IBM' s relational database management system. Data in SQL is retrieved by SAS directly via a set of SAS procedures tailored for use with SQL. This database interface is accomplished via the SAS Institute's SAS/SQL-DS product. The set of data to be modeled as well as models and information about model construction are held in SQL tables.

1. Database Structure for Historical Data

We use SQL/DS to store the data used in the regressions. (See Date[4] for a discussion of relational database in general and the SQL approach in particular.) Two tables contain the historical sales data and header information used as input to our system, and three tables store the system's results. We avoid the overhead of additional software by storing the knowledge system's results in SQL/DS as well. The historical data is stored in table ITEMDATA, using the following structures:

CODE	number identifying each brand item in the database
STORE	number identifying in which store the item was sold
WEEK	time series index
UNITS	number of units sold that week
PRICE	price at which the item was sold
DISP	number of units featured in a display
FEAT	measure of column inches given to the item in an ad feature
REGPRICE	regular price (used to determine price cuts)

Specific CODE and STORE combinations uniquely identify data subsets within the dataset. The CODE field is referenced by the informational lookup table BITEMS (Brand items):

CODE	number unique to the brand item
BRAND	brand name of the item
ATTRIB	a certain feature, such as color or scent
SIZE	unit size

The BITEMS table provides a translation between the easily recognized English descriptions of the brand item and the single CODE the system utilizes. Once the CODE and STORE combination is selected, the system retrieves that data subset and runs the model results, which are saved in an SQL database prior to the next iteration of the system.

2. Modelbase Structure

After the coupled system builds a model, the results of the analysis need to be stored for convenient access at a later time. The statistical results are one of two types: model specific or coefficient specific. Model parameters such as R^2 have one value per model while parameters such as the t-statistic have values for each variable in a model.

We use this distinction between the model results to define the relationships in the relational table structures. Given key fields to relate the tables to one another, we create a record in a table (LOGENTRY) to store the reports on the expert system's failure to finalize a model, or records in tables for storing the model parameters (MODEL), and the variable parameters (ELASTS). LOGENTRY is defined with the following structure:

CODE	refers to a brand item, as in the data table
STORE	refers to the store selling the item, as in the data table
MODELNUM	code assigned to keep track of which model was run
RUNDATE	time-stamp of when the model was run
MESSAGE	the reason a model was not generated

MODELNUM and RUNDATE are the key fields relating to MODEL and ELASTS. When the system returns a proper model for a complete data subset, the regression is run and the model results stored in MODEL, in the following columns:

CODE	refers to brand item, as in the data table
STORE	refers to the store selling the item, as in the data table
MODELNUM	code identifying the model type
RUNDATE	time-stamp of when the model was run
RSQUARED	first of the fields storing statistics: R-squared
DURBWATS	Durbin-Watson statistic
SSE	sum of the squared errors
MSE	mean of the squared errors
CF	the model's certainty factor

To store the results specific to each term of the model, ELASTS has been constructed:

CODE	refers to a brand item, as in the data table
STORE	refers to the store selling the item, as in the data table
MODELNUM	code identifying the model type
RUNDATE	time-stamp of when the model was run
COEFF	name of the model term
VALUE	parameter estimate
STERR	standard error of the estimation
SIGNIF	level of statistical significance of the parameter
CF	certainty factor of the parameter
OK	"T" if the value of CF refers to the confidence in the term

The three previous tables form the M^2KS's modelbase. To view an example, if one iteration generated a model consisting of a constant term, price-cut term, and display term, then LOGENTRY receives no record, and MODEL would hold the model parameters:

CODE	87570
STORE	120
MODELNUM	3
RUNDATE	876268800
MODEL	MODEL = PRICE DISPLAY / NLAG = 0
RSQUARED	.6478
DURBWATS	1.5806
SSE	10509.4900
MSE	214.4793
CF	78

ELASTS would also be updated with new data:

```
CODE              87570
STORE               120
MODELNUM              3
RUNDATE      876268800
COEFF          INTERCPT
VALUE           44.177
STERR            1.764
TSTAT           25.037
SIGNIF          0.0000
CF                  86
OK                   T
```

Similar records would be generated in the elasticities table for the price-cut and display terms of the model. The three records in ELASTS are keyed to MODEL via the fields MODELNUM and RUNDATE, and the data subset on which the regression was run is identified by the fields CODE and STORE. The chart below shows the relationships between the two SQL/DS tables that store the historical data (BITEMS & ITEMDATA) and the three SQL/DS tables that store the model results model (LOGENTRY, MODEL & ELASTS).

```
BITEMS    ITEMDATA    MODEL       ELASTS      LOGENTRY

CODE ---- CODE ------ CODE ------ CODE ------ CODE
BRAND     STORE ----- STORE ----- STORE ----- STORE
ATTRIB    WEEK        MODELNUM .. MODELNUM .. MODELNUM
SIZE      UNITS       RUNDATE ... RUNDATE ... RUNDATE
          PRICE       MODEL       COEFF       MESSAGE
          DISP        RSQUARED    VALUE
          FEAT        DURBWATS    STERR
          REGPRICE    SSE         TSTAT
                      MSE         SIGNIF
                      CF          CF
                                  OK

-----   Data subset relationships
.....   Model number relationships
```

This implementation of table structures is the most efficient way to store model results. It also allows easy access to the data by different analysis systems for problem spotting, causal analysis, and updating of model formulas.

THE OPERATING SYSTEM

The knowledge system, the statistical system, and the database manager are all running under the VM/CMS operating system. Communication between the virtual machines running the knowledge system and the statistical system is accomplished through the use of CMS and CP.

1. IBM' s Conversational Monitor System (CMS)

CMS handles file creation and maintenance in M^2KS. Both the knowledge system and the statistical system can read and write their own CMS files; they also have the ability to read each other' s files. This is one of the chief means of passing data between the two systems in the prototype.

For example, the knowledge system tells SAS what data to retrieve from SQL by writing a CMS file describing the data it wants; SAS reads the file and retrieves the data the knowledge system requested. From SAS' s side, when SAS has finished running a numerical analysis, it writes its results to a CMS file, which the knowledge system reads; the knowledge system can incorporate SAS' s results into its own knowledge base and use those results for further reasoning.

2. IBM' s Control Program (CP)

CP is the common base under which all virtual machines in the CMS system operate. In addition to communication via the CMS file system, another means of communication between the ESE machine and the SAS machine is via CP' s Inter-User-Communications Vehicle (IUCV). The IUCV allows programs running in the two machines to communicate with each other directly by using special message facilities.

For example, if the knowledge system wants to start a SAS program, it sends the SAS machine a message via CP. When the SAS system is finished running its analysis, it sends a message back to the ESE machine via CP to let the knowledge system know that it is done.

EXAMPLE APPLICATION

As discussed in the last chapter, our initial coupled system implementation serves to estimate a marketmetrics model of a single brand item using a model of the following form:

$$UNITS = B_0 + B_1{*}PRICECUT + B_2{*}DISPLAY + B_3{*}FEATURE + E$$

where

```
UNITS = weekly retail sales in units
PRICECUT = regular price - shelf price
DISPLAY = level of in-store displays
FEATURE = retail ad features in newspapers
          (column inches)
E = random disturbance term.
```

Although this is a very simple model, it is used here to illustrate the principles and operation of coupled systems. The data for this model are scanner data for the light duty detergent category in one market.

When estimating and evaluating this type of model, the marketmetrician goes through a series of steps involving data retrieval, preliminary data analysis, initial model estimation, model criticism, and model refinement. The M^2KS duplicates these steps, as shown below.

Data Retrieval. M^2KS extracts data from SQL/DS for a particular brand item. The SAS/SQL-DS software produces a SAS dataset containing week, units, regular price, shelf price, display, and ad features.

Data Check. The system checks to see that the dataset exists, has sufficient observations, contains no holes (missing data), and has sufficient variation in each of the causal factors.

Initial Model Construction. Based upon the initial data check, the system formulates a linear model, as shown above, which contains the causal factors that pass the data check for sufficient observations and sufficient variation.

Initial Model Estimation. Ordinary Least Squares is used to estimate the initial model.

Autocorrelation Detection. One of the problems with time-series data is autocorrelation or serial correlation in the disturbance term (E). M^2KS detects first-order autocorrelation via the Durbin-Watson test.

Autocorrelation Correction. The system uses SAS' s PROC AUTOREG to estimate the model if autocorrelation has been detected. The Yule-Walker equations are utilized to estimate the equation. An iterative procedure is used to arrive at the length of the disturbance lag structure. This procedure starts with a first-order assumption and increases the length until an insignificant autoregressive parameter is detected.

Model Storage. The final model is stored in two tables in SQL-DS via the SAS/SQL-DS software.

These various steps account for the currently implemented Generalized Modeling Procedure. Clearly, other aspects of marketmetrics could be implemented, such as tests and procedures for multicollinearity, heteroscedasticity, and lagged variables.

COUPLED SYSTEMS NARRATIVE

This narrative follows one iteration of the modeling process through its five major phases: getting data to model, checking the data to see if it is suitable for modeling, running the model, checking to see if the model correctly described the data, and saving the model and its output.

The interaction between SAS and ESE in the five-phase modeling process is shown in the following figure and summarized below:

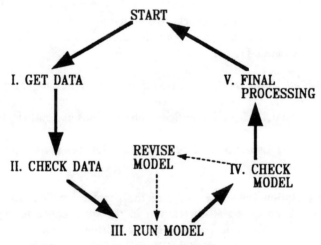

Figure 7.5. The Five-Phase Modeling Process

```
I.  GET DATA TO MODEL
     1. ESE ASKS the user what data to analyze.
        WRITES a file: The requested data.
        TELLS SAS: Get the data from SQL.
     2. SAS READS ESE's file: The requested data.
        DOWNLOADS the data from SQL.
```

    CHECKS the data for holes.
    WRITES a file: Data description.
    TELLS ESE: OK.
  3. ESE CHECKS: Did SAS write a file describing the data?

II. CHECK THE DATA: SUITABLE FOR MODELING?
  1. ESE READS SAS's file: data description.
     CHECKS for sufficient variation in the data.
     If insufficient, STOP.
     ASSIGNS certainty factors to the model terms based on
       the data check.
     CONSTRUCTS a model and assigns it a certainty factor.
     WRITES a file: Description of the model terms.
     TELLS SAS: Get the description of terms.
  2. SAS READS ESE's file: Description of the model terms.
     TELLS ESE: OK.

III. RUN THE MODEL
  1. ESE WRITES a file: The model.
     TELLS SAS: Run the model.
  2. SAS READS ESE's file: The model.
     RUNS the template program, using ESE's model to
       analyze the data.
     WRITES a file: Results of the model run.
     TELLS ESE: OK.

IV. CHECK THE MODEL: DID IT DESCRIBE THE DATA?
     ESE READS SAS's file: Results of the model run.
     CHECKS the results. IF the results are:
       OK: Continue.
       NOT OK: Revise the model and go back to step III
         to rerun.
       NOT OK AFTER 3 REVISIONS: STOP.

V. FINAL PROCESSING
  1. ESE WRITES a file: The final model.
     TELLS SAS: Run the model.
  2. SAS READS ESE's file: The model.
     RUNS the final model to get the final results.
     UPLOADS model and results to SQL.
     TELLS ESE: OK.

Though the modeling process revolves primarily around ESE and SAS, three
virtual machines are used to complete the task: one running the expert system
(ESE), another running the statistical system (SAS), and a third running the

database (SQL). In addition, several other software components are used by the coupled system, as described below.

Communication between the ESE and SAS machines is achieved in two ways: via the message facility of the control program (CP) and via the file handling resources of the CMS operating system, which allows file sharing between machines.

CMS's REXX control language controls the flow of processing within the SAS machine, handles file management by issuing CMS commands, and performs certain utilitarian tasks not suited to SAS, such as parsing files. The controlling REXX exec is the front-end between SAS and any special messages sent to the SAS machine. The REXX exec is also in charge of directing CP to send confirmation messages back to the ESE machine when SAS processing is complete.

Five Pascal-language procedures allow ESE external access: to read and write CMS files, to execute CMS commands, and to participate in CP's message system.

SQL handles the data in tables and is accessible directly from within SAS and also from REXX.

CONCLUSION

This chapter has described an applied architecture for coupling a knowledge system to an information system. The concepts and procedures used in coupling IBM's Expert System Environment with SAS can be applied to couple ESE with other information systems. And, the marketmetrics application is just one of many types of analysis that could be implemented via coupled systems.

The key criteria for such coupling seems to involve problem-solving behavior in which it is not possible to specify in advance the paths one will have to take in the analysis. A common starting point with new data may reveal a new pattern, which causes the user of the information system to request a new view of the data. This new view may trigger new thoughts and require yet other requests of the information system. The result is a large combinatorial situation that makes AI a useful approach.

This type of analysis is common in the field of marketing where a manager has to understand the performance of hundreds of items in dozens of markets. Manufacturing offers a similar environment when the production process involves a large number of components supplied by many vendors and used in multiple processes. Coupled systems offer one way to off-load this detective work to an expert system.

NOTES

1. McCann, John M. *The Marketing Workbench*, Homewood, IL: Dow Jones-Irwin, 1986, p. 198.

2. Gladd, N. T., and N. A. Krall. "Artificial Intelligence Methods for Facilitating Large-Scale Numerical Computations," in *Coupling Symbolic and Numerical Computing in Expert Systems*, J. S. Kowalik (Ed.) Amsterdam, North Holland, 1986, pp. 123-36.

3. REXX is a control language for writing CMS control files; these files are similar to PC DOS BAT files.

4. Date, C. J. *An Introduction to Database Systems, Volume I*, Third Edition, Reading: Addison-Wesley, 1981.

CHAPTER 8

MODEL ANIMATION

INTRODUCTION

The Marketmetrics Knowledge System can be used to build a modelbase containing marketmetric models at the store, chain, or market level for all items or brands. The procedures for such model specification, estimation, and testing are well developed and the literature in this area is voluminous. But, very little work has been done in the area of model presentation. Given that a model has been successfully developed, how are the results best presented to a manager? Can the model be presented in such a way that the implications of the model are self evident to the manager who does lacks a deep understanding of models and would not know how to interpret or apply the model? This chapter describes an exploration of these types of question.

Models are developed and used for different purposes, such as understanding, control, forecasting, and planning. The first two purposes focus on the use of the model to understand and analyze history; the latter two purposes involve the future. The following provides an example of each purpose:

Understanding. Use the model to gain an understanding of the forces that have been affecting an item' s performance.

Control. Use the model to measure the return on investment of the various marketing elements and programs.

Forecasting. Use the model to forecast the most likely performance levels.

Planning. Use the model to evaluate the probable impact of different marketing programs and competitive environments.

In all of these cases, the manager would like to interact with a metaphor or image of the model. That is, a mathematical model needs to be presented in a form that is amenable to understanding and absorption by the viewer.

The model is a representation of a manager's world. Consider a a simple world involving a brand in a local market. A manager interacts with the world by actually observing the world or taking measurements of the world. In this case, the manager could make regular visits to stores in the market and observe the increased sales due to the promotion. Or the manager could view data and graphs that measure sales levels before, during, and after the promotion. In this case, the manager thinks about the world through filters and viewing mechanisms. S/he takes various measures on the world and displays these measures to understand the performance of the world. These displays are the manager's metaphors or images.

The challenge for the modeler is to display the model using the same metaphors. The philosophy would be to let people view the model of the world with the same types of displays that they use to view the world. For instance, a manager of new products may use a graph of unit sales versus time as a means of displaying and understanding a new product's performance. A model of this performance should display its results using the same type of graph. In this way, the manager does not have to learn a new way of viewing the world.

Animated has been defined[1] as "endowed with life or the quality of life." We define *model animation* to be the act of "giving life to a model." Clearly, a model presentation that causes the manager to think that s/he is interacting with his/her normal measure of the world would be animated. It would be endowed with the quality of life. It would not have to look like the actual world; it would have to have the look and feel of the manager's normal metaphors of the world.

The next section describes the modeling context, followed by a discussion of the models being animated. Then the methods for model animation are described. The following section discusses the software procedures. The resulting system is then described. The final section presents a discussion of future approaches.

MODEL CONTEXT

Marketing data based upon UPC scanners and in-store measurements are becoming available from data vendors such as A.C. Nielsen and SAMI/Burke. These data include weekly measures on units sold, price, displays, and retail advertising. It has been shown that statistical models can effectively capture the relationships between units and the causal factors of price, display, and advertising. Wittink. et al.[2] and Blattberg and Wisniewski[3] are two recent demonstrators of such modeling.

Shown in figure 8.1 are graphs of units, price, display, and retailer advertising for one brand in one chain for one year. The price graph contains a solid, irregular line near the top of the graph, which is an inferred regular price line. This line was inferred from an algorithm that examined the current data value and compared it with data from the past eight weeks. The maximum during the eight-week period was taken to be the regular price for the brand.

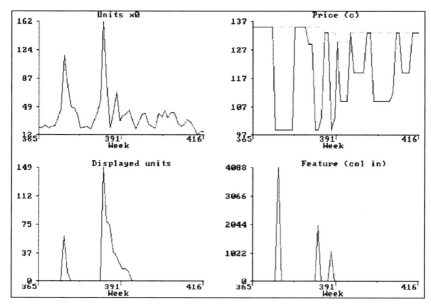

Figure 8.1. Causal Factor Data

A manager or analyst would examine these data and make observations like the following:

These data clearly show that units sales are influenced by price, features, and advertising. There are two periods of major sales increase in the first half of the period. Examination of the other three graphs indicate that these two periods were characterized by price cuts, display activity, and feature advertising. The unit sales graph for the latter half of the period, after about week 395, shows some more modest sales increases. The other three graphs indicate that these increases are associated with modest price drops but neither display and feature activity were present during these periods. Finally, the sales seem to return to a baseline when all merchandising activity ceases; this baseline is around 200 units/week.

This causal analysis provides the manager with an understanding of which marketing variables (price, display, and feature) were present or absent when sales increased over the baseline. This level of analysis does not allow the manager to infer the relative importance of the various variables; such an inference does not seem possible using only the manager's cognitive skills. Models are clearly required.

The Marketmetrics Knowledge System could produce these models and store them in a modelbase for use by the manager. The following represents a simple[4] model of the relationship between units and the three causal factors shown in figure 8.1.

$$\text{units}_t = a + b*(\text{regular\_price}_t - \text{price}_t) + c*\text{display}_t + d*\text{feature}_t \quad \text{(Eq. 8.1)}$$

where **a**, **b**, **c**, and **d** are parameter estimates, regular_price$_t$ is the item's regular price during week t, price$_t$ is the actual price, display$_t$ is the size of the display space allocated to the item during week t, and feature$_t$ is the size of the retailers' newspaper advertisements during week t.

The estimation of this equation using the data in figure 8.1 via ordinary least squares produces results shown in figure 8.2.

coeff.	value	st. error	T-stat	signif.
CONSTANT	209.9973	18.5701	11.3084	0.0001
PRICE	761.5987	100.2434	7.5975	0.0001
DISPLY	4.4668	0.6100	7.3226	0.0001
FEATURE	0.1240	0.0258	4.8062	0.0001

PALMOLIVE Coefficient List

Model: UNITS=a+b(REGP-PRICE)+cDISP+dFTR

R-squared: 0.8719
Durbin-Watson: 1.8900

Figure 8.2. Typical Regression Package Output

These are the types of results that managers find hard to comprehend and utilize; they must be brought alive for them. One approach is to apply the model to produce results in a form that matches a manager's normal metaphors.

The model animation system allows us to convert the model output shown in figure 8.2 into business graphs like those shown in figure 8.1. Managers have a long history of viewing and interpreting line graphs. The remainder of this chapter goes through the output of the model animation system to tell the story of the impact on the three marketing causal factors on unit sales. It provides an answer to the question, What was driving this brand item? The model animation system applies a very simple but powerful idea: Simulate the historical impact of each of the causal factors using the model estimates in figure 8.2.

Equation 1 is solved for each week for which there is data in the database to estimate the total units sold in each week. And, it is also used to produce estimates of the units sold each week due to a price cut, the display activity, and the feature activity. For instance, units sold in week t due to display activity are obtained from Equation 1 by setting regular_price$_t$ = price$_t$, feature$_t$ = 0 to produce the equation:

$d$units$_t$ = **a** + **c***display$_t$ (Eq. 8.2)

Similar substitutions are used to produce equations for units due to price activity (called punits$_t$) and units due to feature activity (called funits$_t$).

$p$units$_t$ = **a** + **b***(regular_price$_t$ - price$_t$) (Eq 8.3)

$f$units$_t$ = **a** + **d***feature$_t$ (Eq. 8.4)

The constant term, **a**, as an estimate of brand equity.

For every week, the model animation system obtains the item data from the database and estimates of the parameters **a**, **b**, **c**, and **d** from modelbase, and uses these data and equations 1-4 to estimate the total unit sales as well as the units attributable to each of the causal factors. Since these causal factors represent retailer merchandising activity, the remainder represents the sales attributable to the brand' s equity.

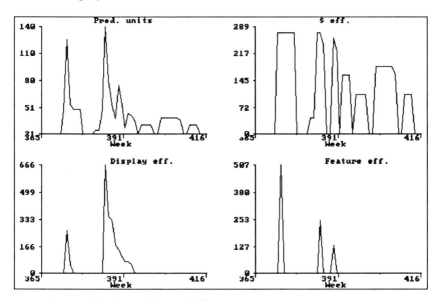

Figure 8.3. Causal Factor Effects

Figure 8.3 contains graphs of these four simulated series. The graph in the upper-left corner contains the total contribution of all the factors; it is obtained by substituting actual values in equation 1. The other three graphs show data produced by equations 2, 3, and 4. For instance, the price effect graph in the upper-right corner shows an estimate of the number of units that were sold each week due to deviations of actual price from regular price.

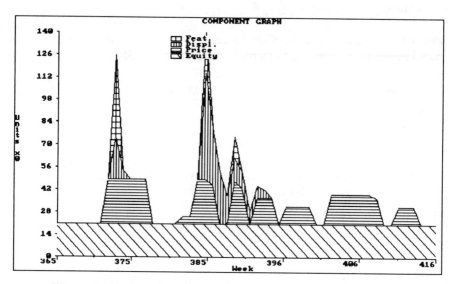

Figure 8.4. Summation of Causal Factor Effects

Figure 8.4 contains the data generated by equations 2, 3, and 4 superimposed on one graph, along with the constant term in the model. This one graph is the key one in the model animation system because it allows a manager to obtain a clear view of the relative impact of the various factors on the brand. It allows the manager to obtain an answer to the question, What's driving my brand? An answer is obtainable for each week during the historical data period.

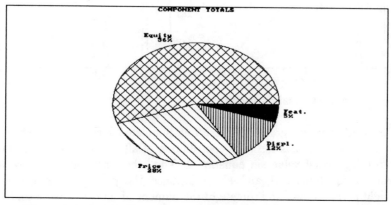

Figure 8.5. Total Effects of Causal Factors for Year

Figure 8.5 contains a pie graph that sums the data in figure 8.4 for the entire year. The pie graph shows that price discounting is estimated to have accounted for 28% of the year' s unit volume, followed by display and then features. In total, chain merchandising efforts accounted for 44% of the item' s volume. Although these figures contain a very simple application of models, managerial reaction[5] indicates that most managers have not been exposed to these types of data or graphs. They have only seen graphs like those in figure 8.1 that only show the data.

A MODEL-BASED PROMOTION REVIEW

This section describes one use of the model animation system: identifying unique retail promotion periods and estimating the relative impact of the causal factors during each promotion. Looking ahead, this section serves as a springboard for the topic of the next chapter — the use of knowledge-based systems for reviewing the impacts of promotions. This knowledge system automatically applies the data analysis and reasoning that is unveiled in the remainder of this chapter.

Reviewing the impact of promotions is an increasingly important part of marketing in the consumer packaged goods industry. Models such as PROMOTER[6] provide a modeling and measurement system for such analysis. A methodology for the identification and analysis of trade promotions based upon a sales response model for the item being promoted will be described. We illustrate the approach by working through an example session with the system.

As with the PROMOTER model, the first step in promotion analysis is the identification of a promotion period. By examining figure 8.1, a manager could detect a trade promotion lasting for one week or more by observing abnormal sales levels or the existence of one or more promotion variables. If during any given week sales were up significantly *and* price was lower than normal *and* a display existed *and* a feature existed, then the manager could be certain that a sales promotion was in effect in the chain. If only some of the conditions exist, the manager could still conclude that it was a promotion week, but perhaps with a lesser degree of certainty in the conclusion. If similar conditions exist for sequential weeks, then the manager could infer the presence of a multiweek promotion.

Figure 8.1 shows that these conditions existed for multiple weeks clustered around week 390. By changing the graphing interval (See figure 8.6), a clearer view of this promotion period can be obtained. The manager can see that the promotion seems to have begun in week 382 with a small price drop, and ended in week 395 when price returned to normal, there were no display or feature activities, and sales returned to the base level.

Repeated application of this process would reveal the existence of six unique promotions. It should be noted that this method does not always produce unambiguous identification of promotion periods. Examination of figure 8.6 shows that during weeks 387 and 388 price returned to normal levels and ad features were not used, resulting in a return of unit sales to the baseline level. An analyst **could** decide that the promotion was over, even though there was still significant display activity in the chain. Or, the analyst could conclude that the continuation of the display activity was sufficient to allow weeks 387 and 388 to be considered promotion weeks, and thus result in a continuous promotion period during weeks 382−395.

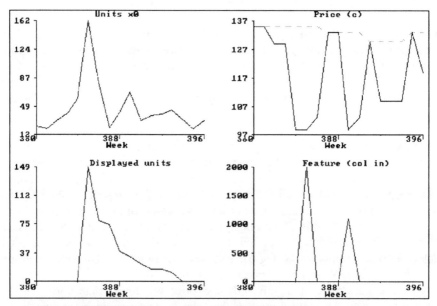

Figure 8.6. Causal Factor Data for One Promotion

Such analysis completes the first phase of a typical two-part promotion review: the identification of promotion periods. The next phase is the measurement of the impact of the promotion on sales during each of these periods. This could be accomplished by redrawing figures 8.4 and 8.5 over each promotion period.

Figure 8.7 shows estimates of the weekly incremental volume during weeks 382−396 due to price, display, and feature obtained from equations 2, 3, and 4. Figure 8.8 reports estimates of the total incremental volume produced by each of these causal factors during the promotion period.

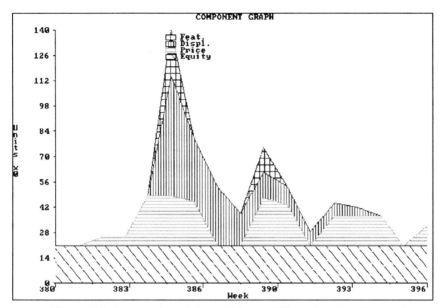

Figure 8.7. Summation of Causal Factor Effects for One Promotion

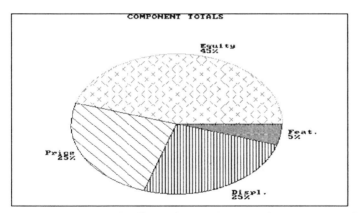

Figure 8.8. Total Effects of Causal Factors for One Promotion

CONCLUSION

Our initial foray into model animation has demonstrated that the results of models can be brought to life by presenting the results of a historical simulation in graphical form very similar to the graphs managers use to view data. Informal discussions with marketing managers and analysts indicate that the graphical approach to this problem serves to bring alive the models in a way that matches their mental models used to view data. Since data are viewed via graphs, putting model results into the same format seems to lead to acceptance of the model.

This work allows one to identify hypotheses about managerial use of models that could be tested by behavioral research paradigms. Such studies would then lead to better design of model animation techniques. The current model animation system could be considered the beginning of a research stream rather than the end product of a research program. In a sense, it provides the basis for study of mental models being employed by managers when they think about markets and marketing programs.

NOTES

1. **Webster' s Ninth New Collegiate Dictionary,** Merriam-Webster Inc., 1985.

2. Wittink, Dick R., Michael J. Addona, William J. Hawkes, and John C. Porter. "SCAN*PRO: A Model to Measure Short-Term Effects of Promotional Activities on Brand Sales, Based on Store-Level Scanner Data," Working Paper, May, 1987.

3. Blattberg, Robert C., and Kenneth J. Wisniewski. "Price Induced Patterns of Competition," Working Paper, University of Chicago, September, 1986.

4. Equation 1 is a very simple model used for illustrative purposes. Any response function form could have been used.

5. This result is not based upon a scientific study; rather it was obtained from informal discussions with about ten marketing managers over a one-year period.

6. Abraham, Magid M., and Leonard M. Lodish. "PROMOTER: An Automated Promotion Evaluation System," *Marketing Science*, Vol 6, No 2, Spring, 1987, pp. 101-123.

CHAPTER 9

THE PROMOTION DETECTIVE

INTRODUCTION

The last chapter ended with the discussion of the way a manager could use a model-based model animation system to review a brand's performance. This review focused on the identification and analysis of the marketing events that affected the brand. Even with a system like the one in the last chapter, this type of review becomes a costly endeavor because of the number of promotions implemented in any one year.

This chapter describes one approach to replacing the human analyst with a knowledge-based system. A common analysis involves a review of an item's promotion history over an annual time period. This review requires the manager to identify each promotion and measure its impact on sales or profits. THE PROMOTION DETECTIVE is a prototype system for doing this review.

Systems like the Marketmetrics Knowledge System could produce models required for the review and store them in an SQL relational database system. THE PROMOTION DETECTIVE would access these models and the data required for the review.

OVERVIEW

THE PROMOTION DETECTIVE is a knowledge-based system that conducts a promotion review of a brand item. Such a review is done in two stages. During the first phase of a promotion review an analysis of the data is conducted from a promotion-spotting perspective. The goal of this stage is to find promotional weeks and to report on the nature of these promotions. If a manager were faced with this task, s/he could then compare the expected results of a promotional program to the actual promotional behavior or story. This leads to the second stage of a promotion review.

If large deviations from the expected were found, the manager would seek an explanation for the abnormal behavior. The second stage thus calls for a problem-spotting perspective by which promotional periods are further analyzed for problems or abnormalities. Moreover, this second stage calls for an explanation of these aberrations.

In phase 1, THE PROMOTION DETECTIVE methodically searches through the data looking for promotional weeks. The data that is trolled by the system is weekly scanner data at the chain level (data aggregated at the store or market level could be used as well). These data are supplemented with causal variables such as display and ad features; the gauges of promotional activity. If, for example, in observing week 382 the system sees that Kroger sold an unusually large number of jars of 8 oz. Jif crunchy peanut butter, and that the item was featured in Kroger' s weekly flier, it would note that week 382 was a promotional week. After all weeks are analyzed, the system becomes a reporting device that collects, calculates, and tabulates numbers that are based on the model of the brand item.

At this point THE PROMOTION DETECTIVE' s user decides if the system should look for abnormalities. If further analysis is needed, phase 2 is initiated. The system delves more deeply into the data in an effort to investigate the types of problems that THE PROMOTION DETECTIVE knows about. The current version of THE PROMOTION DETECTIVE performs an analysis that explains why display activity can taper off during the course of a multiweek promotion.

A SAMPLE SESSION

THE PROMOTION DETECTIVE is a multiphase system in the sense that it executes distinct modules in sequence. There are two main phases:

Phase 1. Promotion Identification and Quantification
Phase 2. Problem Detection and Analysis.

In Phase 1, THE PROMOTION DETECTIVE examines each week for which there is data on the item in the database and classifies it as either a promotion or a nonpromotion week. In this regard, THE PROMOTION DETECTIVE is similar to the PROMOTER[1] system, which executes a similar task. THE PROMOTION DETECTIVE takes advantage of the certainty factor facilities of expert system shells to record a degree of certainty that the week is actually a promotion week. For instance, if it only observes a large sales increase but no pricing, display, or feature activity, it is only 50% certain that a promotion was in effect. This certainly increases with the number of causal factors present during the week.

After each week has been classified, THE PROMOTION DETECTIVE uses the item's response function to produce estimates of the number of units attributable to each causal factor. The equations and procedures for this stage of the analysis was presented in the last chapter.

For every promotion week, THE PROMOTION DETECTIVE obtains the item's data from the database and the sales response function from a modelbase, and uses these data and model to estimate the total unit sales as well as the units attributable to each of the causal factors.

At this point in THE PROMOTION DETECTIVE's work, it has identified promotion weeks and used the model to produce summary statistics for each of those weeks. Since actual promotions usually run for multiple weeks, the next step is to identify promotion **periods**. THE PROMOTION DETECTIVE does this by looking for continuous promotion weeks. If it has identified five consecutive weeks as promotion weeks and if these weeks are preceded and followed by a nonpromotion week, it will identify these five weeks as a promotion period. It then uses each week's summary statistics to produce corresponding summary statistics for each promotion period.

The following screen shows the results of phase 1 for 22 ounce, clear Palmolive.

```
           MODEL INTERPRETATION FOR PALMOLIVE

 1. A PROMOTION OCCURRED BETWEEN WEEK 372 AND WEEK 377
 2. A PROMOTION OCCURRED BETWEEN WEEK 382 AND WEEK 394
 3. A PROMOTION OCCURRED BETWEEN WEEK 396 AND WEEK 399
 4. A PROMOTION OCCURRED BETWEEN WEEK 402 AND WEEK 408
 5. A PROMOTION OCCURRED BETWEEN WEEK 411 AND WEEK 413
 6. EXIT


 WHICH OF THE ABOVE MULTIWEEK PROMOTIONS DO YOU WANT TO VIEW?
    2_
```

The screen shows the result of THE PROMOTION DETECTIVE's methodical search through the weekly scanner data for a Palmolive brand item. THE PROMOTION DETECTIVE has not only identified individual promotional weeks but has aggregated these weeks into multiweek promotion periods. In this example case, THE PROMOTION DETECTIVE has identified five distinct promotional periods. Choosing one of these periods allows the manager to examine a summary of the promotional behavior for the multiweek period. This summary is based on the numbers estimated in the sales response function of the item. If period 2 is selected the following screen appears:

```
┌─────────────────────────────────────────────────────────────────────┐
│                                                                       │
│                 MODEL INTERPRETATION FOR PALMOLIVE                     │
│                                                                       │
│   IN REVIEWING THIS BRAND'S SALES AND PROMOTION HISTORY THE FOLLOWING  │
│   OBSERVATIONS CAN BE MADE ABOUT HOW MUCH EACH PROMOTIONAL TOOL        │
│   CONTRIBUTED TO SALES DURING THIS 13-WEEK PROMOTION:                  │
│                                                                       │
│   PREDICTED SALES WERE 7017.71 UNITS                                   │
│                                                                       │
│   DISPLAY ACTIVITY ACCOUNTED FOR 29.75 % OF SALES                      │
│                                                                       │
│   FEATURE ACTIVITY ACCOUNTED FOR 4.33 % OF SALES                       │
│                                                                       │
│   PRICE-CUTTING ACCOUNTED FOR 28.63 % OF SALES                         │
│                                                                       │
│   EQUITY OR BASELINE SALES ACCOUNTED FOR 37.30 % OF SALES              │
│                                                                       │
└─────────────────────────────────────────────────────────────────────┘
```

This screen shows what we mean by a brand's promotional behavior. The gauges of promotional behavior chosen for this application were display, feature, and price-cutting. These are the causal or explanatory measures. This output shows that almost 30% of the brand item's predicted unit sales were accounted for by display activity, for example. The manager can also note that featuring this item was not very effective and that price-cutting contributed nearly as much as did displaying the brand item. These percentages are based on the elasticities of the three causal variables that are estimated by the model for this Palmolive item, and the degree to which these causal factors were operating during this 13-week promotion.

Phase 1 is primarily a reporting phase in the sense that THE PROMOTION DETECTIVE uses promotion detection heuristics and a sales response function to identify promotion periods and to produce a report summarizing the source of volume during each period. Given this foundation, THE PROMOTION DETECTIVE can then move on to the analysis of interesting aspects of each promotion period.

In designing THE PROMOTION DETECTIVE, we were faced with the question, What is an interesting aspect of a promotion? Our answer was to identify aspects of the promotion period that are abnormal or unexpected. This led to the question, What would be expected? Expectations can flow from empirical results, theory, or typical industry practices. In the former case, similar analyses could have been performed on many items or the same item in different markets. Whenever a result is obtained that deviates significantly from the past results, this deviation can be further analyzed and reported to the manager. For instance, past results may show that, other things being equal, ad features are more effective at generating sales than displays. If the reverse is true for the item under review, then THE PROMOTION DETECTIVE could be programmed to contain the appropriate knowledge base.

The retail industry tends to follow certain practices, and deviations from these practices might be interesting to the manager. For instance, it is somewhat common that when a retail chain decides to install a special display for an item, it instructs all its stores to install the display for the length of the promotion period. The expected display pattern would look like a step-function where display activity goes from zero to some level for the number of weeks of the promotion and then returns to zero again. Deviations from such a pattern would indicate that this practice was not being followed. And, further analysis of the situation could result in deeper insight into the problem.

THE PROMOTION DETECTIVE knows about 1) display practices like those shown in the above graph, 2) how to detect deviations, and 3) how to do additional analysis to find the underlying reason for the unexpected pattern. This display analysis is triggered via the following menu:

```
1. DISPLAY ANALYSIS

2. NO FURTHER ANALYSIS

SEE WHICH OF THE ABOVE FOR THIS MULTIWEEK PROMOTION?   1
```

By choosing display analysis, the manager initiates THE PROMOTION DETECTIVE's second phase. In this mode THE PROMOTION DETECTIVE's reasoning process looks for problems with the promotional variable of interest and analyzes the problem.

```
DISPLAY ACTIVITY TAPERED OFF DURING THE COURSE OF PROMOTION.

WOULD YOU LIKE TO OBSERVE THIS GRAPHICALLY?   YES__
```

THE PROMOTION DETECTIVE has found a problem with the displaying of this Palmolive brand item during this multiweek promotion. The problem is that the chain did not display the brand consistently during the 13-week period. A manager reviewing the effectiveness of a past promotion would probably like to know why this has happened. THE PROMOTION DETECTIVE displays the appropriate graph. (See figure 9.1.)

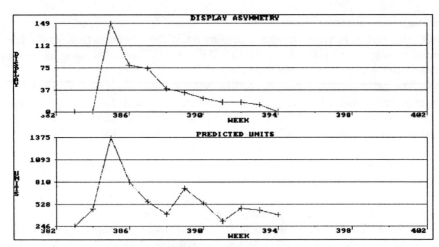

Figure 9.1. Display Activity During Promotion

THE PROMOTION DETECTIVE then sets off in pursuit of an explanation, and displays a screen providing display asymmetry information. (See figure 9.2.)

ONE OF THE REASONS FOR THIS DISPLAY BEHAVIOR IS THAT:

   THE NUMBER OF STORES CARRYING DISPLAYS DECREASED

WOULD YOU LIKE TO SEE THIS GRAPHICALLY?   YES__

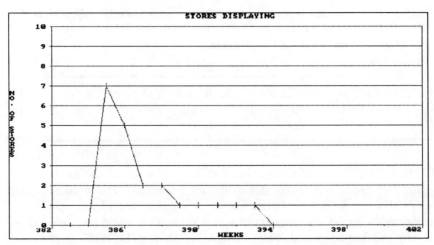

Figure 9.2. Asymmetry in Number of Stores Displaying the Item

THE PROMOTION DETECTIVE's reasoning process has found, out of several possible reasons for the display asymmetry, that the number of stores putting up displays for this brand item decreased as the multiweek promotion progressed. This is illustrated in the preceding graph, which is generated by THE PROMOTION DETECTIVE.

The manager has an option to look at each promotional week in isolation as in the figure below:

```
                    MODEL INTERPRETATION FOR PALMOLIVE

    IN REVIEWING THIS BRAND'S SALES AND PROMOTION HISTORY THE FOLLOWING
    OBSERVATIONS CAN BE MADE ABOUT HOW MUCH EACH PROMOTIONAL TOOL
    CONTRIBUTED TO SALES DURING THIS MULTIWEEK PROMOTION:

       FOR WEEK 385.00

       WEEK 385 WAS A PROMOTIONAL WEEK WITH DISPLAY, FEATURE, AND
       PRICE-CUT WITH A 100.00% DEGREE OF CERTAINTY

       PREDICTED SALES WERE 7017.71 UNITS

       DISPLAY ACTIVITY ACCOUNTED FOR 29.75 % OF SALES

       FEATURE ACTIVITY ACCOUNTED FOR 4.33 % OF SALES

       PRICE-CUTTING ACCOUNTED FOR 28.63 % OF SALES

       EQUITY OR BASELINE SALES ACCOUNTED FOR 37.30 % OF SALES
```

THE PROMOTION DETECTIVE's analysis and summary report aspects are illustrated in the above figure. The numbers on the summary screen are based on the model of the item, so the manager can see how this kind of report further summarizes the data by summarizing the model. In this way THE PROMOTION DETECTIVE allows the manager to have a better feel for the relative impacts of the three promotional tools, and this is what a promotion review should do.

HOW DOES THE PROMOTION DETECTIVE WORK?

In this section we first present an overview of how THE PROMOTION DETECTIVE works. This is a discussion of the expert system shell we used to write the program, GURU, as well as a preview of THE PROMOTION DETECTIVE's components, which include a knowledge system, a procedural language, and a database component. We then proceed to look in more detail at each of these components in turn.

Overview

THE PROMOTION DETECTIVE is composed of a knowledge system and other components needed to make the program work. GURU[2] was selected for the following reasons:

> 1) THE PROMOTION DETECTIVE is a data-oriented expert system so there was a need for easy access to data from the knowledge system. GURU provides this through its relational database component.

> 2) The nature of the problem dictated a procedural component in addition to an expert system. Since THE PROMOTION DETECTIVE's purpose is to review marketing data in search of promotional weeks in order to interpret the model of this data, it should entail a review of one observation of a week's measures at a time. We call this record-oriented reasoning and it implies that the expertise used to flag promotional weeks needs to be applied repeatedly for every week in the data. This calls for an overriding procedure. Such a procedure is easy to create in GURU.

> 3) There was a need for graphics as well graphing options are readily available in GURU.

THE PROMOTION DETECTIVE's design specifications therefore called for three basic components: an expert system shell, a procedural language, and a database system.

Knowledge System Component

The knowledge component consists of two major parts: the knowledge base and the inference engine or reasoning strategy. The knowledge base in GURU is referred to as a rule set. In a generic sense, a rule set consists of a collection of if-then heuristics or rules and a goal variable. Encoded in the rules is a way to find a value for the goal variable, so it becomes the charge of the reasoning strategy to find and follow that path. We first look at the knowledge base part of the knowledge system component.

One of GURU's flexibilities is that many rule sets can be defined for one program. THE PROMOTION DETECTIVE takes advantage of this flexibility in that there are two rule sets that are open for consultation during a session. Having several rule sets allows a developer to compartmentalize the knowledge needed to solve different aspects of one problem.

THE PROMOTION DETECTIVE's ultimate goal is to tell a story about the promotional history of a brand item. To achieve this end THE PROMOTION DETECTIVE is designed to have two subgoals. The first subgoal is the week-by-week, record-by-record analysis of scanner data alluded to earlier. The second subgoal is problem detection and explanation. This second subgoal is represented in THE PROMOTION DETECTIVE by the system's second phase in which problems or abnormalities in display activity are sought.

The week-by-week and display analyses are two different parts of the ultimate goal, but the knowledge needed to reason about them is different so we create a rule set for each aspect. To spot a promotion week, THE PROMOTION DETECTIVE looks at both the outcome variable (unit sales) and the causal factors (price, display, advertising, feature). It has heuristics such as the following:

> If in looking at one week's record you see that unit sales of the brand item are more than twice the average for the whole time period, and that there was some display activity, you can conclude that week was a promotional week with a good degree of certainty.

This heuristic can be represented in a more rulelike fashion with some filtering. You could write the following:

```
IF:     BRAND SALES > 2 * AVERAGE BRAND SALES AND
            DISPLAY > 0

THEN:   WEEK IS A PROMOTIONAL ONE
            WITH SOME DEGREE OF CERTAINTY
```

In fact, with a little modification we can write the GURU version of this rule:

```
IF:     VOLUME > 2 * PUNITAVG AND
            DISP > 0

THEN:   TELLME = "THERE WAS A LARGE VOLUME BOOST
            WITH DISPLAY ACTIVITY IN WEEK ___"
            CERTAINTY __
```

This GURU rule is typical of the fifteen rules in the first rule set that flags promotional weeks.

The move from an Englishlike version of a heuristic to an executable GURU rule is very similar for the rule set that embodies display analysis knowledge. For example, a chunk of knowledge that we have about in-store displaying of merchandise looks like the following:

If display activity has been tapering off during the course of a multiweek, chainwide promotion then it is possible that the number of stores carrying the display decreased correspondingly.

A more succinct version of this piece of knowledge might look this:

```
IF:    DISPLAY ACTIVITY HAS BEEN TAPERING OFF AND
       THE PROMOTION IS A CHAINWIDE ONE

THEN:  THE NUMBER OF STORES CARRYING DISPLAYS
       DECREASED
```

This display analysis knowledge differs from that needed to capture promotional weeks, and the goals that drive these rules are different. Thus the need for different rule sets.

Although the rule sets contain rules with different purposes, the reasoning strategy is the same throughout THE PROMOTION DETECTIVE. Backward-chaining is the inferencing strategy that is used, though the nature of the problem does not preclude forward-chaining. The problem can be examined from two perspectives.

From one perspective, the problem of reviewing marketing data in search of promotional weeks can be treated as a selection problem. There is a finite number of promotional states in any one week. The brand item can be specially priced, displayed, or featured. Any combination of these promotional measures, or none of them, is also feasible. Nonetheless, the number of combinations is small, so the problem is one of *selecting* the appropriate combination or state. From this angle, backward-chaining is the appropriate strategy.

From the other point of view, you can think of the problem as being a data-driven one in which the system extracts a promotional history for a brand item from a large database of numbers. Data-driven problems seem to be more amenable to forward-chaining, so the rule sets in THE PROMOTION DETECTIVE could be reasoned with in this fashion as well.

For THE PROMOTION DETECTIVE the issue of reasoning strategy does not appear to be a very important one. Suffice it to note that we chose the backward-chaining strategy.

The resolution of the goal is sought by looking at two dependencies. If during a particular week there is a sales lift, then there is some evidence that one could classify the period as a promotional period. The second dependency lies between the combination of sales lift and pricing, displaying, and featuring activities, with the period' s classification as a promotional or nonpromotional period. If there is a sales lift accompanied by display, feature, or price-cutting activity then there is even more evidence that the period is a promotional one.

If either of the two dependencies yields the observation that the period is a promotional period, then part of the conclusion is the creation of the data that ultimately tells the promotional story. We will discuss the creation of more data in the discussion of the database component.

Procedural Language Component

The procedural language in GURU was used to do several things. First, it allowed THE PROMOTION DETECTIVE to conduct a methodical search through the weekly scanner data as it reconstructed the promotional history. In particular, the fact that the procedural language contains a traditional looping control structure, among other control structures, allowed THE PROMOTION DETECTIVE to iterate through the data, observation by observation.

A second facet of the procedural language is the concept of a perform file. In GURU a perform file can be used as the main program or as a subroutine. All of THE PROMOTION DETECTIVE' s parts come together in one main perform file.

The procedural part of THE PROMOTION DETECTIVE is a necessary component because it performs those kinds of operations that a knowledge system is not designed to do. Most notably, it creates an access for the rule sets to the data.

Database Component

THE PROMOTION DETECTIVE is a data-oriented knowledge system that need access to weekly scanner data. GURU' s relational database system is the storage location for these data because of its SQL-like query language. This language provided a relatively easy way to complete the critical link between the knowledge system that drives the analysis, and the data that contains the promotion story.
THE PROMOTION DETECTIVE' s database includes 4 tables:

- An ITEM table
- An OBSERVATION table
- A MODEL table
- A STORE table

The table on which THE PROMOTION DETECTIVE's initial attention is focused is the ITEM table. This is the table that contains the weekly information on brand item unit sales, price, display activity, and feature activity, among other variables. A typical record looks like the following:

```
CODE (BRAND ITEM):                      SOAP354
WEEK:                                       385
UNITS:                                     1616
PRICE:                                     0.99
DISPLAY:                    (DISPLAY)       149
MAJORAD:                    (FEATURE)        16
PREDUNIT:                               1374.91
REGPRICE:                                  1.35
```

THE PROMOTION DETECTIVE's week-by-week analysis rule set reasons with these pieces of information for every week in the ITEM table.

One piece of this information is the number of predicted units for the items in each week, which must be calculated from the item's model as shown in equation 8.1. These brand item models are stored in the MODEL table so THE PROMOTION DETECTIVE has easy access to the coefficients and can thus draw on these coefficients to calculate the percentage contribution numbers that the system reports. It is from the MODEL table as well that THE PROMOTION DETECTIVE retrieves the predicted unit values that it uses to fill the predicted units field in the ITEM table.

Looking at the example record from the ITEM table again, one would conclude that week 385 is a promotional week. There is display activity, which is measured by the number of items on display, and feature activity, which is calculated as the number of column inches of advertising in the chain's weekly circular. This brand item's price is quite a bit lower than the regular price as well. THE PROMOTION DETECTIVE would conclude that week 385 is a promotional one as well and would proceed to document this by placing its conclusions in the second table mentioned above: the OBSERVATION table. For each record in the ITEM table there is a corresponding record in the OBSERVATION table. The week-by-week promotion analysis rule set determines what should be in the latter of these two tables. For a brand item with little promotional activity, the second table would be filled with many zeros. For the brand item used above to represent a typical ITEM record the corresponding OBSERVATION record would look like this:

```
                                                385
WEEK:
BOOST:                     WEEK 385 WAS A PROMOTIONAL
                           WEEK WITH DISPLAY, FEATURE,
                           AND PRICE-CUT
DISPCT:                                       51.19
FEATPCT:                                      14.72
PCUTPCT:                                      19.44
PREDVOL:                                    1374.91
CFACTOR:                                        100
MANYPRO:                                          2
ASYMMTRY:                                         0
```

The BOOST field contains the textual conclusion that states that the week is a promotional one.

The DISPCT, FEATPCT, and PCUTPCT variables are percentage figures that refer to how much each of the promotional variables contributed to the PREDVOL (predicted volume) value. These percentages are based on the statistical model as well in that they are based on the coefficients estimated in this model.

The CFACTOR field records the degree of belief that THE PROMOTION DETECTIVE' s rule set has in its conclusion. Since all three promotional tools were used in this case, and the predicted brand item unit volume was very high, THE PROMOTION DETECTIVE is 100% sure of its conclusion. The MANYPRO field refers to whether or not this week belongs to any multiweek promotion period, and if so, of which period it is a member. In other words, if in looking across the whole time frame THE PROMOTION DETECTIVE finds groups of consecutive promotional weeks, it labels these groups and each week within a group, as multiweek promotions.The last field, the ASYMMTRY variable, is one that is filled by the display analysis rule set conclusions. The display analysis rule set is linked however to the last of the three tables; the STORE table.

The STORE table is a disaggregated, but pared down version of the ITEM table. It too has measures of display, feature, and price-cutting activity but these measures are represented at the store level. This table is used by THE PROMOTION DETECTIVE when it searches for the problem of display asymmetry across a multiweek promotion, and the cause of this problem. For every week characterized by display asymmetry THE PROMOTION DETECTIVE places a flag in the ASYMMTRY field of the OBSERVATION table.

DISCUSSION

THE PROMOTION DETECTIVE is similar to the PROMOTER system in the sense that it detects promotions and measures their impact. The two systems start in a similar manner: They examine the data to determine the existence of a promotion. PROMOTER has several characteristics that make it different from THE PROMOTION DETECTIVE. In particular, PROMOTER

- runs on factory shipment data

- requires the brand group to input a promotion schedule, which it uses to determine the existence of a promotion week

- uses exponential smoothing techniques to determine a baseline during the promotion periods by extrapolating smoothed data from nonpromotion periods

- only reports the total impact of each promotion and does not have a means to estimate the relative impact of the various causal factors

- was not built with knowledge-system tools

These differences are primarily caused by the fact that THE PROMOTION DETECTIVE uses a sales response function and PROMOTER does not. THE PROMOTION DETECTIVE assumes that a sales response function has been built and stored in a modelbase for each item that it analyzes. In a sense, this can be considered a very restrictive assumption because most companies do not have these models lying around.

However, various studies (Blattberg and Levin,[3] Blattberg and Wisniewski,[4] and Wittink et al.[5]) have shown that the scanner data permit the development of these models. The Marketmetrics Knowledge System describes a knowledge-based system that could build these models. These results point to the ability of firms to build and maintain the requisite modelbases, which would permit the adoption of systems like THE PROMOTION DETECTIVE.

Several conclusions can be drawn from designing and building THE PROMOTION DETECTIVE. The purpose of the research was to determine whether or not a knowledge-based system could perform a promotional review by searching through scanner data. We believe that the answer to this question is yes.

Translated into an operational goal in the context of The Marketing Workbench, THE PROMOTION DETECTIVE was an attempt at using a data-oriented knowledge system to interpret models of brand item behavior. We think that this attempt was successful. More specifically, we have shown that THE PROMOTION DETECTIVE performs four generalizable functions. It finds promotional weeks, reports promotional results, looks for abnormalities in the promotional results, and explains these abnormalities

This proof-of-concept illustrates that one can represent heuristics in the form of if-then rules to perform the four general tasks embodied in THE PROMOTION DETECTIVE's functions: finding, reporting, looking, and explaining. THE PROMOTION DETECTIVE can be extended by expanding the current functions or adding new functions.

The display analysis knowledge could be widened to cover other potential abnormalities. Or to investigate other possible explanations for the example problem detected in THE PROMOTION DETECTIVE. We used a heuristic that states that one reason that display activity might taper off is that the number of stores in the chain carrying the display decreases as a multiweek promotion unfurls. It is also possible to use a rule that states that if the size of the display decreases while the number of stores remains the same, the display activity would taper off.

In addition to the display analysis rule set that searches for abnormalities in display behavior, THE PROMOTION DETECTIVE could be expanded to include feature and pricing modules that perform similar analyses.

THE PROMOTION DETECTIVE is an example of a larger class of applications which analyze and report on the performance of some marketing entity. In the example in this chapter, THE PROMOTION DETECTIVE analyzes 22 ounce, clear Palmolive in one chain in one market. The same philosophy could be used to generalize the analysis to the brand or category level, to conduct the analysis for all chains in a market, to conduct it at the market level instead of the chain level, etc.

Further, the system has illustrated an approach to using a knowledge-based tool in the analysis of marketing data. It illustrates the notion of having a system examine the data just as a manager would examine it and report its findings. It also illustrates the concept of selective reporting of an abnormality. In this system, it looks for asymmetric promotion performance and points out its existence. In a sense, this is nothing more than an application of the concept of management by exception in that it only reports about situations that are an exception to the norm. But THE PROMOTION DETECTIVE goes beyond this exception reporting in that it knows a reason for the exception and examines additional data (in this case, the store-level data) to locate one or more reasons for the exception.

NOTES

1. Abraham, Magid M., and Leonard M. Lodish. "PROMOTER: An Automated Promotion Evaluation System," *Marketing Science*, Vol 6, No 2, Spring 1987, pp. 101-123.

2. *Guru Reference Manual*, Lafayette, IN: Micro Data Base Systems, Inc., 1985.

3. Blattberg, Robert C., and Alan Levin. "Modelling the Effectiveness and Profitability of Trade Promotions," *Marketing Science*, Vol 6, No 2, Spring, 1987 pp. 124-46.

4. Blattberg, Robert C., and Kenneth J. Wisniewski. "Price-Induced Patterns of Competition," Working Paper, Graduate School of Business, University of Chicago, 1986.

5. Wittink, Dick R., Michael J. Addona, William J. Hawkes, and John C. Porter. "SCAN*PRO: A Model to Measure Short-Term Effects of Promotional Activities on Brand Sales, Based on Store-Level Scanner Data," Working Paper, 1987.

CHAPTER 10

DEALMAKER

Era I, II, and III systems can be thought of as preparatory to the real action: the design of marketing programs. The first three eras involve the *understanding* part of marketing; the fourth era focuses on the influencing aspect of marketing. Era systems assist a marketing manager in the design of the various aspects of a marketing program.

This chapter describes one such system, DEALMAKER, which assists a manager in the design of trade deals. The first section describes the shifting marketing focus to accounts, which increases the need for systems such as this one. The type of knowledge contained in DEALMAKER is described in the next section. The remainder of the chapter presents a sample session with DEALMAKER.

ACCOUNT FOCUS

A change is occurring in some firms with respect to the focus of marketing activities: from the consumer to the customer. A recent magazine article highlights this trend:

> *Which comes first, the retailer or the brand? In the most profound re-evaluation of brand management to date, many consumer-goods companies now say the retailer, and some are beginning to reorganize their marketing departments to prove it.*[1]

This shifting focus leads to emphasis on trade-related programs — programs containing incentives such as case allowances and cooperative advertising. Firms responding to a recent survey[2] of consumer packaged goods manufacturers indicated that they were spending almost one-half of their advertising and promotion resources on trade promotion.

Additionally, there are strong organizational implications of this change because consumer packaged goods firms have been built upon the concept of mass marketing. Mass marketing is just what the phrase says: treating the market as a whole. A market is analyzed to gain an understanding of consumer and competitive behavior. Based upon this analysis, a marketing program is designed and executed against the entire market.

This "nation as the target" philosophy is attenuated via the concept of market segmentation in which the total market may be decomposed into a small number of segments, with each segment approached with a mass marketing philosophy. The key concept of mass marketing is to avoid having to understand any one consumer by treating large collections of consumers as if they are homogeneous.

This practice is required because of the sheer size of the market: over 200 million potential consumers in the U.S. alone. But, how does this philosophy change for firms that have a smaller number of customers? The practices of industrial marketing firms, firms who practice business-to-business marketing, provides the obvious answer. Each customer is treated as an individual. From this perspective, marketing requires an understanding of that individual' s situation and preparation of a marketing and sales program specifically for that customer.

The shifting focus from consumers to retailers is bringing about a similar shift in organizational structures for accommodating the required change in marketing philosophy. Just as IBM treats General Foods as an individual customer, General Foods has to treat Giant Food as an individual customer. When preparing a marketing program, a marketing manager tends to think about the consumer or the target market to denote the collection of consumers in the mass market. A program is prepared for this target; the fact that this program is probably not optimal for most of the consumers is not considered because there are simply too many consumers in the target market to worry about the match between the one marketing program and each and every consumer.

When thinking about the retailer trade, this marketing manager brings to bear the same philosophy: s/he thinks about the trade and prepares a marketing program for the trade as if it were a mass market.

This mass marketing philosophy dissolves when you look at the field sales force, where managers speak of Giant Food, Krogers, Vons, and Kmart. That is, the field sales force treats each retailer as an individual customer. The firm has individuals assigned to each retail account, and may even treat each retail division as a somewhat separate account. But, the field sales force in most firms does not have responsibility and authority to design marketing programs. Their job is to execute the trade aspects of marketing programs that were designed by the brand groups.

The shifting focus to the retailer means that the concept of account marketing is joining the mass marketing concept as an equal partner. But, how does a firm execute account marketing in an organization designed for mass marketing? The obvious answer for some firms is shared marketing responsibility and authority: *share the marketing responsibility between the centralized brand group and the decentralized field sales force.*

The reason for giving account marketing responsibility to the field sales force is easy to understand. The sales manager who has historically been responsible for each account is the one person in the firm with the best understanding of the needs and wants of that firm. Since marketing can be thought of as the process of designing a marketing program that meets the needs and wants of a target market at a desired profit, it is natural to give this sales manager the marketing responsibility at the account level. The sales manager is the individual in the firm who best understands how an account will react to different trade programs. Therefore, it is natural to give this manager the responsibility of designing that account' s trade program.

This organizational design philosophy calls for the placement of the marketing responsibility in the hands of the individual who has the knowledge of the customer. It moves marketing responsibility to the location of the knowledge.

Perhaps a firm could reverse the logic: move knowledge to the location of the marketing responsibility. That is, move knowledge about each account to the brand group. Both of these approaches are efforts to manage the complexity of having to attend to more detail in the design and implementation of marketing plans. The former approach is an arms and legs effort aimed at placing more people (the field sales force and other groups with regional marketing responsibility) at the focal point of the problem. The later is an attempt to centralize the firm' s knowledge of individual account differences to aid in understanding and managing this complexity by a smaller number of individuals.

MARKET MODELING

The concept of moving knowledge of account practices to the brand group can be considered in the somewhat larger context of modeling a market. The changing focus means that the brand group needs to plan, execute, and control marketing programs that take into consideration the retail trade. It does not necessarily mean that the retailer will become the entire center of focus and that the consumer will not be considered. A balanced view requires the brand group to consider both the retailer and the consumer.

We consider a market to be composed of multiple manufacturers serving multiple retailers, with each retailer serving a consumer base. The manufacturers design trade programs for the retailers. The retailers and the manufacturers design marketing or merchandising programs for the consumers. These relationships are shown in figure 10.1.

This figure contains the various marketing elements that the manufacturers include in their trade and consumer programs, as well as the elements available to retailers in their merchandising programs.

This type of arrangement exists in all markets. If the brand group plans at the Area of Dominant Influence (ADI) level, approximately 200 plans would need to be produced. Such planning is clearly beyond the means of a small brand group, typically consisting of 2-4 people. To make it possible to do this type of work, this brand group would need to be supported by a Marketing Decision Support System (MDSS), which leverages the brand managers' time and efforts. A knowledge-based approach to MDSS design is one means of providing such leveraging.

Alter[3] provides a taxonomy of the roles of decision support systems. One role is to provide a simulation of the impact of decisions. Hence a logical role of an MDSS is to simulate the impact of marketing decisions on the various elements of the marketing channel. Such an MDSS could simulate the impact of marketing programs on the retailers and consumers in a market.

Simulations are built upon models of the elements of the world being simulated. In our case, the system would include retailer and consumer models. Hence the problem of moving knowledge to the brand group requires the firm to capture this knowledge in the form of models and to place these models in an MDSS.

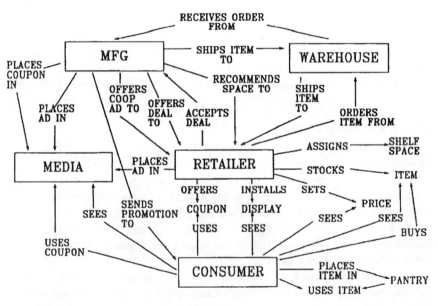

Figure 10.1. A Model of a Market

CONSUMER MODELING

The marketing community has a long history of modeling the impact of marketing elements on consumer purchasing. Econometric models usually serve to quantify the relationship between sales and marketing factors. Naert and Leeflang[4] provide a good overview of such modeling, and Wittink et al.[5] present a recently developed model of the impact of merchandising variables on brand sales. Such models are well developed, and the Wittink paper indicates that they provide a good representation of consumer response to a retailer' s merchandising efforts.

Hence econometric models provide the appropriate representation for capturing and using the firm' s knowledge about consumer response to marketing and merchandising efforts.

ACCOUNT MODELING

Econometric models of an entity are possible when the firm has a sufficiently large database on the entity and the elements that affect that entity. This is the case when one is using scanner data to model consumers' response to retail merchandising. Scanner databases provide weekly data on units sold, price, advertising, and in-store display activities.

But, most firms have not been systematically collecting data on the retailers' response to its trade promotions. Hence, it is usually not possible to use econometric techniques to build an empirical model of a retailer. One study has been reported of the use of econometric models for retailer modeling. Frank and Massy[6] built econometric models of both the consumer response to retailer actions and the retailer response to manufacturer actions and offers. They report success in the consumer modeling and are more guarded in their evaluation of the use of econometrics in retailer modeling. The problem of limited data seems to have been influential in their work.

Other methods and knowledge sources must be found. There is a history in marketing of using managerial judgments in lieu of data to parameterize a marketing model. Consider a model of the form

units = aPb,

where P denotes the price of an item and a and b are constant parameters. The econometric approach involves using data on units and price in conjunction with a statistics package to estimate the unknown parameters a and b. In situations where adequate data are not available, Little[7] proposed the use of managerial judgments: Ask a manager to provide estimates of the parameters a and b. Considerable research has been conducted in this area, and it has been generally concluded that managers are not able to provide accurate estimates of such model parameters.[8]

This decision calculus approach used the same models as the econometric approach but substituted judgment for data. Another approach involves the use of managerial judgment but without the mathematical models.

As was stated earlier, the field sales manager is the individual who possesses the firm' s knowledge about the probable reaction of a retailer to a trade deal. This manager knows the retailer merchandising policies and practices. Years of experience with retail buyers and merchandisers has allowed such a sales manager to gain an intuitive or formal understanding of the heuristics and procedures being used by his or her customer. By capturing and representing this knowledge of retailer practices in the MDSS, the firm will be able to simulate the reaction of each retailer to a trade deal.

The field of artificial intelligence has provided frameworks for encoding knowledge about many phenomena, and these frameworks were thought to be useful in an MDSS. This chapter contains an exploration of the use of AI approaches to representing and reasoning with knowledge of retailer practices.

IMPLEMENTING DEALMAKER IN GOLDWORKS

DEALMAKER attempts to model the components of a market and the relationships among the components. It is meant to capture a marketing or sales manager' s mental model of a market. It can be used in much the same way a manager uses his own mental model: to run marketing experiments and see the results before having to implement them in the real world. It allows him to devise a promotion plan and explore the consequences of implementing that plan in several different markets. Stated simply, the marketing manager gets a system that assists him in answering the question, What happens if I offer this deal for this brand item? Of course, by repeatedly asking this question for a variety of deals in different markets, the brand manager is able to determine an overall marketing plan.

A solution provided by this system is presented in the form of two summaries. One is a view of how successful the overall plan is across all markets. This summary includes information on the nature of the deal offered in each market, the number of chains that considered the deal, the number that accepted the deal, and how much revenue was generated for the manufacturer.

The second view is a view within one particular market, allowing the brand manager to see how individual retail chains responded to the deal. Response here means an indication of whether a retailer accepted the deal, what price was set for an item, a display size, and advertising size.

The most important perspective in this system is that of the manufacturer. The view of the world that a user of this system sees is meant to reflect the needs, motivations, and concerns of the manufacturer. Most of the knowledge embedded in the system, however, is knowledge about the expected behavior of the retailers and consumers.

The system contains a representation of a market that simulates 1) the interactions between a manufacturer and the retailers and 2) the retailers and consumers in the markets of concern to the manufacturer. We use object-oriented programming techniques to implement the framework for the simulation system. The basic objects represented include the markets, the retailers, the consumers, the brand items being sold, and the promotional devices available to the manufacturer. The model of the market has a symbolic and a numerical component. Symbolic modeling is present in the form of forward- and backward-chaining rules used to model the behavior of a retailer. The numerical component of the system is in the mathematical models of consumer behavior within a market.

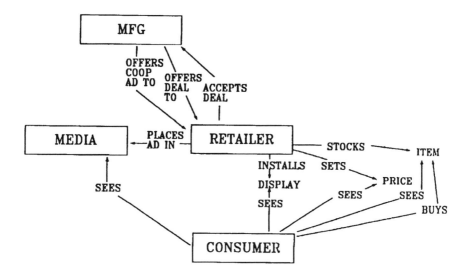

Figure 10.2. The Market Model That Underlies DEALMAKER

In the most general sense, DEALMAKER demonstrates how artificial intelligence programming tools can be used to combine two distinct types of knowledge of local market behavior:

1. Quantitative knowledge of consumer behavior in local markets (that is, econometric models of consumer responses to promotional prices, advertising, and in-store displays of specific brand items in local markets).

2. Qualitative knowledge of retailer responses to trade promotions (that is, the type of knowledge possessed by the field sales force about the behavior of individual retailers in specific markets).

As a prototype system, DEALMAKER has focused on a specific subset of this environment, which is shown in figure 10.2. Knowledge takes many forms in our system. The two most important kinds of knowledge are 1) the knowledge of how retailers respond to deals offered by manufacturers, and 2) how a retailer's actions affect the consumer. In this section we will present a brief description of each of these.

DEALMAKER presents a view of the world to a brand manager that consists of three markets: Los Angeles, Boston, and Chicago. Within each of these markets, there are 2-3 retailer chains. Some chains do business in more than one market. There are three distinct retailers represented in this system. Their philosophies and practices with respect to reacting to deals offered by the manufacturer are given below. These descriptions are based upon interviews with eight grocery and drug retailers.

R1: This retailer always accepts a deal for a brand that is one of the top three brands in the category; otherwise, it is rejected. All deal items get featured, but no displays are used.

R2: This retailer always accepts the deal, but what is done with it is based upon coop advertising dollars. If the deal includes coop money, the retailer will accept the deal and pass on all of the discount to the consumer. If the discount is greater than 30%, he will put up a big display. Otherwise, the retailer leaves the item at regular price and does not use an ad feature or a display.

R3: This retailer's goal is to get low prices; any deal will be accepted and the full case allowance will be passed onto the consumer through lower prices. If the discount is greater than 25% and the item is in the top 50 usage categories, the promotion will include a feature ad and a display. However, this retailer will not accept any deals that have performance requirements.

Each of these statements reflects a different approach for determining a response to deal offer. A rule representation is used to encode this knowledge. There is one rule-set for each retailer.

A retailer's actions have a direct effect on consumer behavior. The mathematical models we use to explain consumer behavior were derived using statistical techniques. The function for consumer response to a deal is a function of three variables: the price-cut (P), the feature level (F), and the display level (D). A simple linear model is used.

$$\text{Units} = c_0 + c_1{}^*P + c_2{}^*F + c_3{}^*D \quad (\text{Eq. 10. 1})$$

c_0, c_1, c_2, and c_3 are parameters that were derived using econometric analysis of the observed values of units and P, D, and F.

The model contains knowledge about

Three fictitious local markets.   These are identified as Los Angeles, Chicago, and Boston.

Seven local chains. There are two chains each in Los Angeles and Boston, and three chains in Chicago.

Seven brand items.   Four of these fictitious brands are in the coffee category, one is a gelatin dessert, and two are breakfast cereals.

Trade promotions.   Trade promotions, or deals, consist of incentives to retailers in the form of case allowances and coop advertising allowances. Deals can also contain performance requirements such as minimum orders, and advertising and display requirements.

Retailer responses to trade promotions.   These responses take the form of promotional pricing, in-store displays, and advertising. Each retailer has a set of policies and philosophies that govern their response to various trade promotions. Some of these policies are global, such as never accepting a trade promotion that has performance requirements. Others are specific to particular levels of incentives and individual product categories.

Consumer behavior.   This knowledge is in the form of econometric models of the effect of price cuts, in-store displays, and advertising features on units sold. As retailers respond to trade promotions by setting prices and engaging in other promotional activities, the environment for consumers changes. Econometric models provide estimates of consumer purchasing behavior as these conditions change.

A SAMPLE SESSION WITH DEALMAKER

The user of the system is intended to be a brand manager charged with designing trade promotions. In the course of completing this task, he or she will use a system screen to design a deal and offer it to all or a selected subset of the available markets. Models of the retailer response and the consumer response are used to simulate the impact of the deal. These models are stored in a mainframe modelbase and downloaded at the appropriate point in the session.

Another set of screens allows the user to review the response to the deal by retailers and consumers. The model can then be queried and explored to better understand why the market responded as in did. This process allows the brand manager to reformulate the deal to reflect this new understanding. The cycle continues until a satisfactory deal has been developed. The manager interacts with DEALMAKER through menus, as shown in figure 10.3.

Figure 10.3 displays the system' s opening screen, a presentation of a menu bar along the top of the screen, and a box labeled *Overall Response to Deal*. The *Overall Response* screen is used to summarize the response of all markets represented in the system to the set of promotional deals currently offered. As no deal has been designed and offered yet, the values of the various market descriptors are filled with zeros.

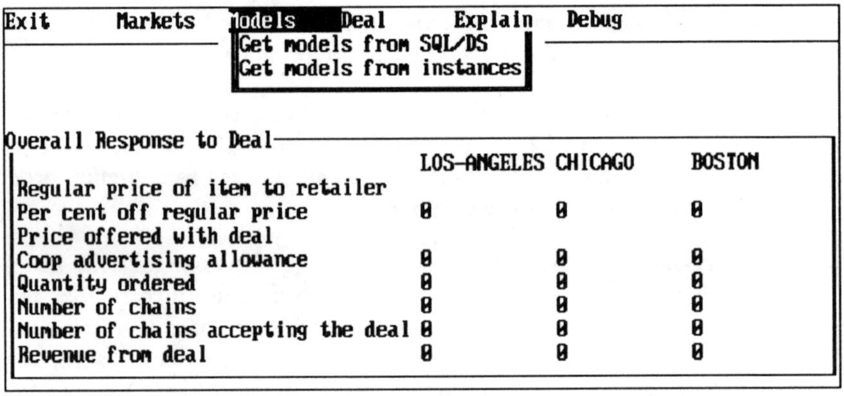

```
Exit       Markets    Models    Deal      Explain   Debug
                     ┌──────────────────────────┐
                     │Get models from SQL/DS     │
                     │Get models from instances  │
                     └──────────────────────────┘

Overall Response to Deal─────────────────────────────────────────────
                                LOS-ANGELES  CHICAGO      BOSTON
Regular price of item to retailer
Per cent off regular price       0           0            0
Price offered with deal
Coop advertising allowance       0           0            0
Quantity ordered                 0           0            0
Number of chains                 0           0            0
Number of chains accepting the deal 0        0            0
Revenue from deal                0           0            0
```

Figure 10.3. Opening Screen and Menu Bar

Notice the *Overall Response to Deal* box includes a summary of each of the local markets: Los Angeles, Chicago, and Boston. For each of these markets, the screen provides information about

The regular price of the item being offered to the retailers. (The system has knowledge of regular prices for each item and retailer).

The percent off regular price (case allowance) accompanying the deal.

The price of the item offered to the retailers with the stated case allowance included.

The percent of coop advertising allowance (if any) provided in the deal. (This is stated in terms of percentage of advertising costs reimbursed).

The quantity ordered by the retailers in response to the deal.

The number of chains operating in the market.

The number of chains in the market accepting the deal.

The revenue generated by the deal in each market.

The remainder of this chapter describes a scenario of how a manager would use DEALMAKER to 1) design a deal, 2) learn of the predicted response of the retailers and consumers to the deal, 3) query the system to understand why the retailers responded as they did, and 4) alter the deal to obtain the desired response.

The *Menu to Define a Deal* screen is used by the deal designer to structure the offering to the trade. When the manager selects Grinder' s Choice 1-LB coffee as the deal item, the list price of the item is automatically filled in on the *Menu to Define a Deal* screen. (See figure 10.4.) Then the user defines the deal, in this case offering a 20% case allowance and a 50% coop advertising allowance. Retailers accepting the deal will be required to advertise Grinder' s Choice with a small ad.

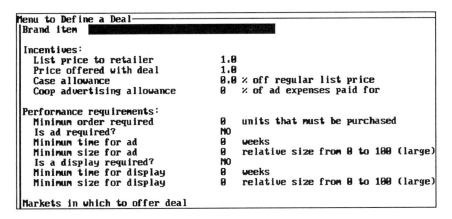

Figure 10.4. Defined Deal

Figure 10.5 displays *Overall Response to Deal* by summarizing the reactions in Los Angeles, Chicago, and Boston. Both retailers in Boston accepted the deal, and one retailer each in Los Angeles and Chicago failed to accept. Also shown in figure 10.5, the user has moved the pointer to the *Markets* menu, and selected *Los Angeles* to begin an inquiry about retailers in this market and their response to the offer. The manager can offer this deal to any set of the available markets. In this scenario, the manager chooses *All Markets* from a menu, denoting the desire to offer the deal in all of the markets.

```
Exit     Markets   Models    Deal      Explain    Debug
         Overall Response
         BOSTON
         CHICAGO
         LOS-ANGELES
Overall R
                                    LOS-ANGELES CHICAGO    BOSTON
         Regular price of item to retailer 1.29      1.29       1.29
         Per cent off regular price         20        20         20
         Price offered with deal            1.03      1.03       1.03
         Coop advertising allowance         50        50         50
         Quantity ordered                   301       678        678
         Number of chains                   2         3          2
         Number of chains accepting the deal 1        2          2
         Revenue from deal                  310.03    698.34     698.34
```

Figure 10.5. The Market's Response and Selecting Los Angeles for Review

Figure 10.6 displays *Response to Deal in Los Angeles*. For both of the retailers (labeled R1-M and R3), a variety of information is provided regarding the ways in which they responded to this offer. The manager is curious about retailer R1-M, and asks for information about R1-M.

```
Exit      Markets    Models    Deal      Explain    Debug



Response to Deal in LOS-ANGELES
                                    R1-M       R3
         Was deal accepted?         YES        NO
         Quantity ordered on deal   301        0
         Regular price of item      1.38       1.38
         Promotion price for item   1.29       1.38
         Price cut from regular price 0.09     0
         Relative size of advertising 10       0
         Relative size of display   0          0
         Predicted consumer demand  335        230
```

Figure 10.6. Los Angeles's Response and Selecting Retailer R1-M

Figure 10.7 displays the system's response. Here, the general set of policies that guide retailer R1-M is displayed in a window; this retailer will accept any deal for top brands in the categories carried. Promoted items are advertised, but apparently no food items are displayed in the store.

At this point, the user wishes to inquire as to why retailer R3 failed to accept the offer. The manager uses a series of steps to obtain a general explanation about retailer R3's acceptance of the deal. (See figure 10.8.)

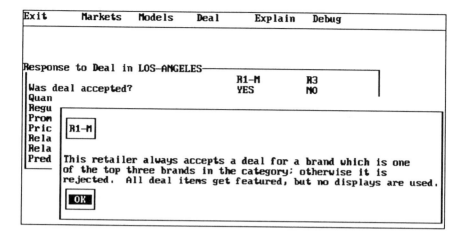

Figure 10.7. The System's General Description of Retailer R1-M

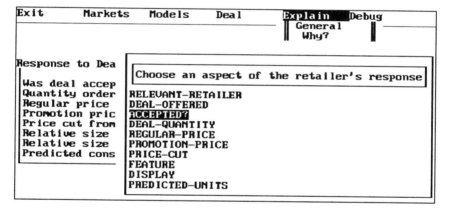

Figure 10.8. Specific Inquiry About R3's Acceptance

Figure 10.9 provides a somewhat cryptic explanation. The message is partly in English and partly in the system's own internal language, due to the prototype nature of the application. However, it is sufficiently clear that one can understand that this retailer rejected the deal because there was an advertising requirement.

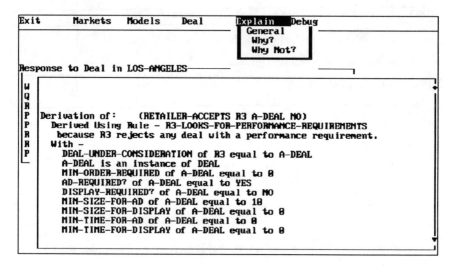

Figure 10.9. The Explanation of R3's Rejection of the Deal

Following this inquiry, the user is also curious about the price point of $1.29, which Los Angeles retailer R1-M has set for Grinder's Choice coffee on this deal. The brand manager would like to have gotten a deeper price cut to the consumer, and uses the system's "Why Not" facility to inquire why a retail price of $.99 was not set by retailer R1-M. The explanation displayed in figure 10.10, is again in a mixed form, containing both English and some internal system language.

```
Exit      Markets    Models    Deal      Explain  Debug
                                         General
                                         Why?
                                         Why Not?

Response to Deal in LOS-ANGELES─────
                                   R1-M          R3

The value 0.99 was rejected as a solution because it failed the following test
(CONSIDER-MARGIN-TARGET CONSIDER-MFG-PRICE)

CONSIDER-MARGIN-TARGET
 A good promotion-price is one that allows a margin target to be met.
CONSIDER-MFG-PRICE
 Reject any promotion-price that is less than the manufacturer's price
```

Figure 10.10. The Explanation for Missing the Desired Price

However, it is revealed that there are two primary reasons for not achieving this deep of a cut. First of all, this retailer seems to have some target margins that need to apply on promoted merchandise, and the $.99 price point would violate those margins. More importantly, however, this deep of a price cut would require that the retailer sell the merchandise below the price offered by the brand manager in the deal. Hence the last line of the explanation: "Reject any promotion price less than the manufacturer's price."

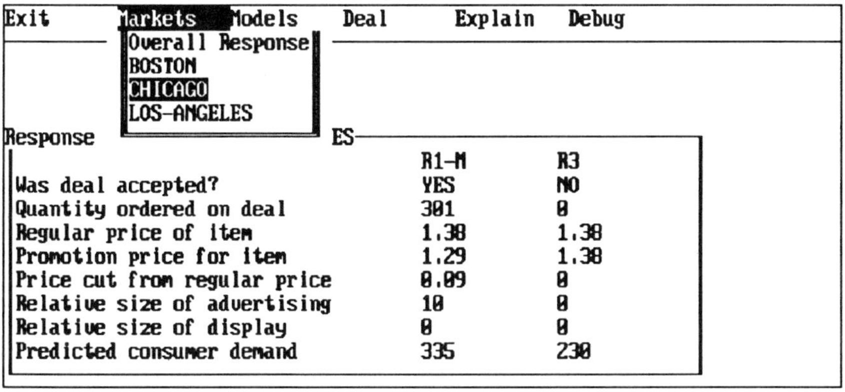

```
Exit      larkets    lodels   Deal     Explain  Debug
         ┌─────────────────┐
         │Overall Response │
         │BOSTON           │
         │CHICAGO          │
         │LOS-ANGELES      │
Response └─────────────────┘ ES
                          R1-M           R3
Was deal accepted?        YES            NO
Quantity ordered on deal  301            0
Regular price of item     1.38           1.38
Promotion price for item  1.29           1.38
Price cut from regular price  0.09       0
Relative size of advertising  10         0
Relative size of display  0              0
Predicted consumer demand 335            230
```

Figure 10.11. Asking to Review the Chicago Response

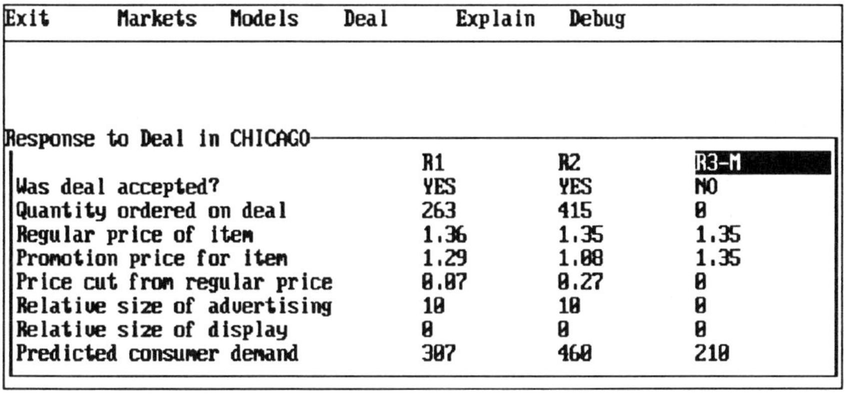

```
Exit      Markets    Models   Deal     Explain  Debug


Response to Deal in CHICAGO
                          R1        R2        R3-M
Was deal accepted?        YES       YES       NO
Quantity ordered on deal  263       415       0
Regular price of item     1.36      1.35      1.35
Promotion price for item  1.29      1.08      1.35
Price cut from regular price  0.07  0.27      0
Relative size of advertising  10    10        0
Relative size of display  0         0         0
Predicted consumer demand 307       460       210
```

Figure 10.12. Inquiring About Chicago Retailer R3-M

Having completed a review of Los Angeles retailers in figure 10.11, our brand manager turns to Chicago. And, figure 10.12 displays the system's summary of responses from retailers in that market. Here retailer R3-M has rejected the deal, while the other two retailers have accepted. In this figure, the pointer is placed on retailer R3-M to obtain an overview of this retailer's policies relative to trade promotions.

Figure 10.13 describes this retailer in terms of the types of items promoted, how they are promoted, and under what conditions deals are rejected. It appears, from this general description that the inclusion of performance requirements may have lead to the rejection of our brand manager's promotion. In figure 10.14, the Markets menu is selected, and a request is made to review the behavior of the Boston retailers. Both chains have accepted the deal in Boston, and the details of their responses are provided in figure 10.15.

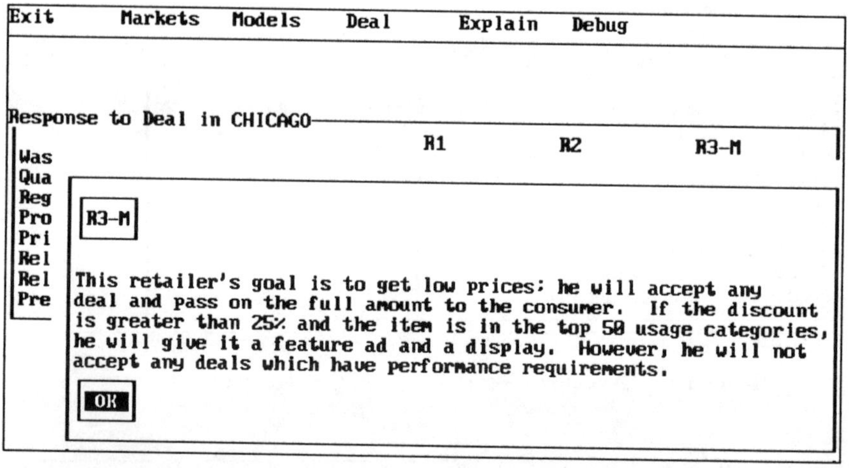

Figure 10.13. The System's Description of Retailer R3-M

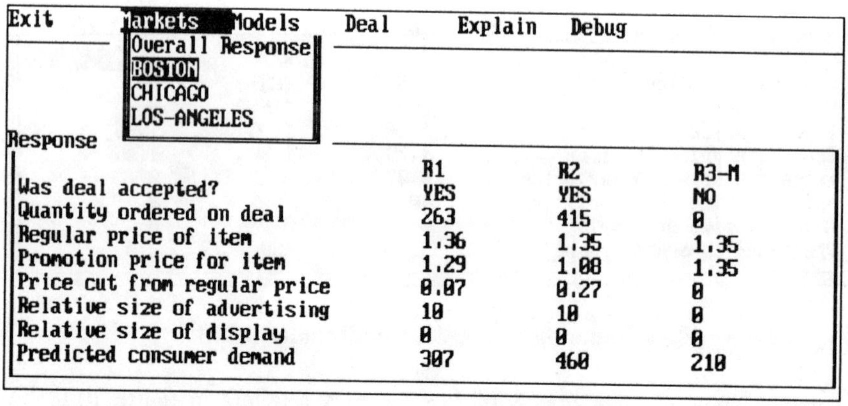

Figure 10.14. Asking to Review Responses of Boston Retailers

```
┌──────────────────────────────────────────────────────────────────┐
│Exit        Markets    Models     Deal      Explain   Debug         │
│                                                                    │
│                                                                    │
│┌Response to Deal in BOSTON─────────────────────────┐              │
││                                  R1         ▐R2-M▌              │
││Was deal accepted?               YES         YES                 │
││Quantity ordered on deal         269         409                 │
││Regular price of item            1.49        1.49                │
││Promotion price for item         1.39        1.19                │
││Price cut from regular price     0.1         0.3                 │
││Relative size of advertising     10          10                  │
││Relative size of display         0           0                   │
││Predicted consumer demand        329         469                 │
│└──────────────────────────────────────────────────┘              │
└──────────────────────────────────────────────────────────────────┘
```

Figure 10.15. Boston' s Response and an Inquiry Regarding
R2-M

A relatively strong response was obtained from retailer R2-M. The user selects that retailer in order to better understand the policies that were in effect when his promotion was evaluated. The description the system has provided is reproduced in figure 10.16. Having learned something about the strengths and weaknesses of the deal as constructed, our new brand manager chooses to restructure his deal. (See figure 10.17.)

In figure 10.18, the deal is redefined to provide a deeper case allowance (30%), and the requirement to advertise has been dropped. Near the bottom of the screen, All Markets is selected as the target of the newly formulated deal.

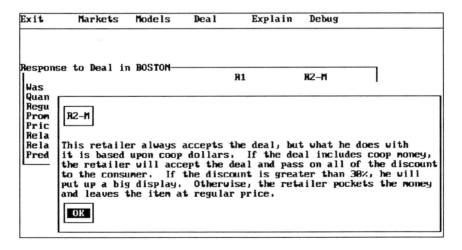

Figure 10.16. What the System Has to Say About R2-M

```
Exit       Markets    Models    Deal      Explain   Debug
                                ┌─────────────────┐
                                │Define a Deal    │
                                │Offer a deal     │
                                └─────────────────┘

┌Response to Deal in BOSTON─────────────────────────────────────┐
│                                    R1            R2-M          │
│Was deal accepted?                  YES           YES           │
│Quantity ordered on deal            269           409           │
│Regular price of item               1.49          1.49          │
│Promotion price for item            1.39          1.19          │
│Price cut from regular price        0.1           0.3           │
│Relative size of advertising        10            10            │
│Relative size of display            0             0             │
│Predicted consumer demand           329           469           │
└───────────────────────────────────────────────────────────────┘
```

Figure 10.17. Asking to Restructure the Deal

```
┌Menu to Define a Deal──────────────────────────────────────────┐
│Brand item  GRINDERS-CHOICE-1LB                                 │
│                                                                │
│Incentives:                                                     │
│   List price to retailer           1.29                        │
│   Price offered with deal          0.9                         │
│   Case allowance                   30  % off regular list price│
│   Coop advertising allowance       50  % of ad expenses paid for│
│                                                                │
│Performance requirements:                                       │
│   Minimum order required           0   units that must be purchased│
│   Is ad required?                  NO                          │
│   Minimum time for ad              0   weeks                   │
│   Minimum size for ad              0   relative size from 0 to 100 (large)│
│   Is a display required?           NO                          │
│   Minimum time for display         0   weeks                   │
│   Minimum size for display         0   relative size from 0 to 100 (large)│
│                                                                │
│Markets in which to offer deal                                 │
│   ----                         ┌─────────────┐                 │
│   OK                           │ALL-MARKETS  │                 │
│   ----                         │BOSTON       │                 │
│                                │CHICAGO      │                 │
│                                │LOS-ANGELES  │                 │
│                                │Retract Value│                 │
│                                └─────────────┘                 │
└───────────────────────────────────────────────────────────────┘
```

Figure 10.18. A New Deal to Be Offered to All Markets

The markets' responses are summarized in figure 10.19. Some improvements have been found, as all retailers have accepted the deal. However, our brand manager notes that even though this is the case, the Boston market is not ordering in large enough quantities to satisfy his objectives. In one final attempt to improve his deal's performance, he returns to the deal construction screen in figure 10.20. Here he places a new restriction on the deal, that a minimum of 500 cases be purchased, and directs this revision only to the Boston market.

Figure 10.21 displays the results. Boston retailers have accepted the deal even with this new requirement, and the quantities ordered have improved accordingly.

```
Exit        Markets    Models    Deal        Explain    Debug
                                │Define a Deal│
                                │Offer a deal │

Overall Response to Deal
                                    LOS-ANGELES CHICAGO      BOSTON
Regular price of item to retailer    1.29        1.29        1.29
Per cent off regular price           30          30          30
Price offered with deal              0.9         0.9         0.9
Coop advertising allowance           50          50          50
Quantity ordered                     1082        1192        783
Number of chains                     2           3           2
Number of chains accepting the deal  2           3           2
Revenue from deal                    973.8       1072.8      704.7
```

Figure 10.19. Market's Response and Another Request to Alter the Deal

```
Menu to Define a Deal
Brand item  GRINDERS-CHOICE-1LB

Incentives:
  List price to retailer         1.29
  Price offered with deal        0.9
  Case allowance                 30    % off regular list price
  Coop advertising allowance     50    % of ad expenses paid for

Performance requirements:
  Minimum order required         500 units that must be purchased
  Is ad required?                NO
  Minimum time for ad            0     weeks
  Minimum size for ad            0     relative size from 0 to 100 (large)
  Is a display required?         NO
  Minimum time for display       0     weeks
  Minimum size for display       0     relative size from 0 to 100 (large)

Markets in which to offer deal    BOSTON
```

Figure 10.20. A Final Correction to the Deal Structure

```
Exit        Markets    Models    Deal        Explain    Debug


Overall Response to Deal
                                    LOS-ANGELES CHICAGO      BOSTON
Regular price of item to retailer    1.29        1.29        1.29
Per cent off regular price           30          30          30
Price offered with deal              0.9         0.9         0.9
Coop advertising allowance           50          50          50
Quantity ordered                     1082        1192        1014
Number of chains                     2           3           2
Number of chains accepting the deal  2           3           2
Revenue from deal                    973.8       1072.8      912.6
```

Figure 10.21. The Final Result: Improved Performance in Boston

The sample session described here is intended to

Provide a feel for working with a model-based system to support a planning exercise,

Illustrate the accessibility to the user of the underlying model of market behavior,

Demonstrate what is meant by a system serving as a repository for company knowledge about local markets,

Illustrate how users unfamiliar with the specifics of local account policies and practices can begin to understand their impact, and learn to respond to their requirements in planning trade promotions.

The key aspect of DEALMAKER that differentiates it from most simulations is its ability to explain its reasoning. This aspect was illustrated through the *Why Not* facility that was used to learn why retailer R1-M did not offer the consumers a $0.99 price. Such explanation ability is the cornerstone of current expert systems and is one of the key features that differentiates expert systems from traditional programs.

The next chapter provides a detailed description of the technologies used to build DEALMAKER. The chapter discusses the fundamental characteristics of the hybrid knowledge system technology used to develop this prototype, the benefits of model-based reasoning systems, and a more detailed description of the implementation.

NOTES

1. Donahue, Christine, and David Kiley. "Marketers to Focus on Retailer," *Adweek' s Marketing Week*, June 8, 1987, p. 1.

2. "Tracking Trade Promotion' s Place in the Universe," *Adweek' s Marketing Week*, September 5, 1988, p. Promote 4.

3. Alter, Steven L. *Decision Support Systems*, Reading, MA: Addison-Wesley, 1980.

4. Naert, Phillippe, and Peter Leeflang. *Building Implementable Marketing Models*, Netherlands: Martinus Nijhoff, 1978.

5. Wittink, Dick R., Michael J. Addona, William J. Hawkes, and John C. Porter. "SCAN*PRO: A Model to Measure Short-Term Effects of Promotional Activities on Brand Sales, Based on Store-Level Scanner Data," Working Paper, May 1987.

6. Frank, Ronald E., and Massy, William F. *An Econometric Approach to a Marketing Decision Model*, Cambridge: MIT Press, 1971.

7. Little, John D. C. "Models and Managers: The Concept of a Decision Calculus," *Management Science*, Vol. 16, B466-B485, 1970.

8. Chakravarti, Dipankar, Andrew Mitchell, and Richard Staelin. "Judgment Based Marketing Decision Models: An Experimental Investigation of the Decision Calculus Approach", *Management Science*, 25, March 1979, pp. 251-263; and Naert, Philippe A., and Marcel Weverbergh. "Subjective Versus Empirical Decision Models," in *Marketing Decision Models*, R. L. Schultz and A. A. Zoltners (Editors), New York: North Holland, 1981, pp. 99-123.

CHAPTER 11

DEALMAKER:
A MODEL-BASED REASONING SYSTEM

Our initial systems were developed with rule-based knowledge system shells such as IBM' s Expert System Environment, Micro Data Base System' s GURU, and M.1 from Teknowledge. More powerful hybrid knowledge system development tools have recently become available for use in the business computing mainstream, and DEALMAKER has been implemented in this class of tool.

Hybrid tools combine the more familiar rule-based representations of knowledge with other methods, previously only available in esoteric research tools or running only on specialized hardware and software. These include KEE (Knowledge Engineering Environment) from Intellicorp and IBM, NEXPERT OBJECT from NEXPERT, and GOLDWORKS from Gold Hill Computing. While all of these tools offer distinctive features and functions, at their core they are more similar than different.

For the most part, hybrid systems come to life, and demonstrate their most unique contributions when used to implement model-based reasoning systems, such as DEALMAKER. *Model-based reasoning systems are distinguished from strictly rule-based systems by attempting to build an explicit model of the entities, structures, principles of operation, and behavior of some system.* The knowledge in these models is not knowledge of expert problem solving behavior, as is usually the case in rule-based systems, but rather knowledge of a system.

In general, model-based reasoning systems have been applied to create models of physical systems such as electrical circuits, factories, or power plants. The models themselves then provide the basis for developing other, specific knowledge-based applications that reason about the behavior of the model. To continue with the example of a power plant model, once the model is created, other expert system applications can be developed to assist an engineer in making modifications to the system by exploring the behavior of the model under different scenarios, or to assist a power plant operator to make decisions about what to do next and why, under a variety of conditions.

DEALMAKER AS A MODEL-BASED REASONING SYSTEM

As stated before, model-based reasoning systems are distinguished from strictly rule-based systems by attempting to build an explicit model of the entities, structures, principles of operation, and behavior of some system. The hybrid knowledge system development tools used to create models of this sort employ general functions and features such as

Frames and Objects to describe the entities of the model,

Hierarchies and Lattices to describe superordinate and subordinate relationships among the entities,

Object-Oriented Programming techniques to define the ways in which entities behave and influence one another.

A later section describes in detail how these functions and features operate, and how they were applied in the development of DEALMAKER. However, it may be useful for the casual reader if we describe some of the unique aspects of these characteristics of hybrid systems to aid in a general understanding of how DEALMAKER was implemented.

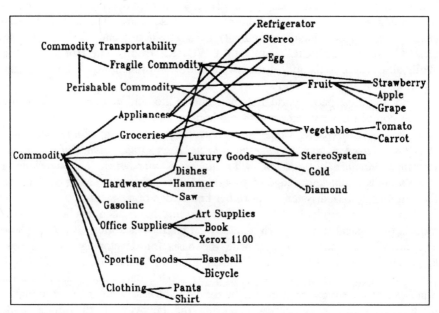

Figure 11.1. Lattice Model of Consumable Commodities

Kunz, Kehler, and Williams[1] have provided a rich discussion of these general characteristics of hybrid systems. One of the key aspects of their concept of a hybrid development system is object-oriented programming, which is described in depth by Stefik and Bobrow.[2] To assist in this overview, the reader is directed to a reproduction of one of their diagrams. (See figure 11.1.)

This diagram depicts the lattice of relationships among several entities in a model of consumable commodities. It can be seen that the system represents these entities as members or instances of higher-level classes. That is, dishes, hammers, and saws are instances, or members of the more general class of hardware. Similarly, eggs and fruit are examples of a more general class of entities, perishable commodities. Whereas eggs are also members of the class of entities, fragile commodities.

DEALMAKER contains a similar structure relating its entities, such as brand items, item categories, trade promotions, markets, retailers, and the like. For example, the system knows that Los Angeles is a market, and that markets have retailers. Similarly, retailers carry brand items, and have policies about trade promotions. Brand items are in categories, which have velocities, and so on.

Once a class of entities has been defined for the system (take for example the class of retailer), adding additional instances, or members of this class is relatively easy. Because the system knows that retailers have a common set of attributes (e.g., numbers of stores, item categories carried, markets in which they compete, average size of stores, numbers of items carried, preferred methods of merchandising), adding an additional retailer to the model is largely a matter of filling in the blanks. In this way, it would be relatively easy to add markets, retailers, brand items, and types of trade promotions to DEALMAKER.

The above description addresses the structure that connects the entities in a model. Another important aspect of hybrid tools is the ability to access object-oriented programming techniques. These techniques provide a means for modeling the ways in which entities behave and influence one another. For example, when a deal is offered, retailers evaluate the deal. If the deal is accepted, promotion prices, and advertising and display levels are set. These values, in turn, influence the quantity of goods ordered, and consumer demand.

Unlike conventional programming languages, these tools are designed to specifically articulate and manage knowledge such as this. An important result of this perspective is that the knowledge is stored in a more accessible manner than in a conventional programming language. It is this feature that allows the brand manager in the scenario presented in the previous chapter to click on Los Angeles, or retailer R1-M, and see this entity, as well as ask about how it got into its current state. Each of the objects or entities has as a part of its definition the ability to display itself, or tell its story. Model-based reasoning systems are really composed of two major parts. One of these is the model itself, built in some hybrid system tool. The other is an application that uses the model.

DEALMAKER is an application designed for a brand manager to structure trade promotions that take into account knowledge of local markets. Other applications could be developed that take advantage of the knowledge stored in the model, however. For example, an application could be developed that would contain some of an experienced brand manager' s knowledge of how to structure trade promotions. Such a system might assist the brand manager by making a good first pass at a promotion, given some particular objectives and constraints. Or, an application could be developed that would monitor the market to determine if marketing plans are playing out as expected and producing desired results.

This type of system provides the following two very important benefits for the management of complex, model-based applications:

1) Models such as these, implemented in this style of programming technology provide a manageable repository for the rich and organizationally dispersed knowledge required to respond to the increasing complexity of marketing decision making.

2) The time required to develop and manage models such as these can be leveraged by the development of additional applications that operate upon and with the model-based knowledge.

BASIC CONCEPTS OF OBJECT-ORIENTED PROGRAMMING

Before beginning the discussion of the implementation of DEALMAKER, we present some introductory material on object-oriented programming. This style of programming heavily influenced the design and implementation of our system. Most of the terms and definitions in this section come from Stefik and Bobrow.

Definition of Terms

Object-oriented programming is a style of programming that combines the descriptions of data and procedure within a single entity called an *object*. It encourages the programmer to concentrate on the data to be manipulated rather than the code that does the manipulation. Object-oriented languages are languages that support this style through predefined features in the language.

An object is the primitive element of object-oriented programming. Each object has a set of operations and a collection of state variables that remember the effect of operations. In object-oriented languages, the term used in place of procedure (or subroutine) call is *message passing*. Message passing is a form of indirect call; you send messages to objects instead of calling procedures. The operation to be performed is named indirectly through a selector, the name of the message, whose interpretation is determined by the class of the object.

Consider the figures below, which are examples from DEALMAKER. The first figure depicts an object named Readi-Food. It has five *slots* which hold the values of the state variables for this object. There are slots to hold values 1) for the items it carries in its stores, 2) for the brands it carries, and 3) for margin targets it has for each category. One slot that has special meaning is the class slot. The class slot indicates that Readi-Food is an object that is one of a larger class of objects called Food-retailer.

```
Readi-Food
Brands-carried       (grinders-choice  magic bean...)
Items-carried        (item1  item2 ...)
Margin-targets       (coffee 0.14  cold cereal 0.08 ...)
Class                Food-retailer
```

One of the most useful aspects of object-oriented programming is the ability to define classes of objects. A *class* is a description of a set of objects that have uniform behavior. Objects of the same class have a common structure (they have the same slots) and have common operations (they respond to the same messages). You can think of a class as a template, a cookie-cutter if you like, from which objects may be created. Another term used in place of class is *frame*, which fits well given this view of a class as a template. The examples we have shown so far have talked about a class of objects called Food-retailer. It is depicted below.

```
Class:      Food-retailer

Slots:      brands-carried
            items-carried
            margin-targets

Messages:   respond-to-deal
            carries-brand
            regular-price
```

Every time you create a new Food-retailer object, or *instance,* this description is used. Each new instance gets three slots and responds to three messages. Each instance carries with it enough space to store values for its state variables. Ultra-Mart is a second instance of the class Food-retailer. Note the structural similarity between this object for Ultra-Mart and the one earlier for Readi-Food. They have the same names for slots because they are both instances of the same class. However, the values stored in the slots are different, reflecting the fact that they are different objects and therefore have different values for their state variables.

```
Ultra-Mart
Brands-carried      (grinders-choice  no-doze-coffee ...)
Items-carried       (item1  item2 ...)
Margin-targets      (coffee 0.14  cold cereal 0.22 ...)
Class               Food-retailer
```

All instances of a class share the same procedures that respond to messages. The procedures are called *methods*, or *handlers*. Earlier we stated that message passing is a form of indirect procedure call. It is indirect because the procedure to be called is determined by looking at the object to which the message was sent. Message passing is a data-driven procedure call. Let us return to our examples to illustrate this. To determine if a particular brand of coffee is carried by the retailer, you would send a message to the object representing the retailer. We depict this process below for two different retailer objects. Each object has its own state variable for brands-carried.

Assume that the message :CARRIES-BRAND causes a retailer object to look on the list of brands it stores in the slot brands-carried. The subroutine that performs the work needed to respond to this message is actually associated with the class of objects to which both Readi-Food and Ultra-Mart belong: Food-retailer. In a Lisp-based system, such as Goldworks, message sending looks like the following:

```
(send-msg 'Readi-Food :carries-brand 'magic-bean)
(send-msg 'Ultra-Mart :carries-brand 'magic-bean)
```

The procedure called is named SEND-MSG. It is responsible for looking at its first argument, the object to which the message is being sent. From an object its class can be determined. Then using the table of methods associated with the class and the message name given (:CARRIES-BRAND in the example above), SEND-MSG calls the method that does the work to determine if MAGIC-BEAN is one of the brands carried. As shown below, Readi-Food indicates that it does carry the item and Ultra-Mart indicates that it does not carry the item.

```
:carries-brand magic-bean => Readi-Food => yes
:carries-brand magic-bean => Ultra-Mart => no
```

The one feature that distinguishes object-oriented programming is *inheritance*. Inheritance is the mechanism that leads to reusability of code. The behavior of a class of objects is defined by means of the messages it supports and the slots in its instances. Inheritance allows you to define new classes in terms of existing classes. Refer back to the description of the class Food-retailer. Every instance had three slots and could respond to three messages. A Food-retailer is really a specialization of a more general class of objects, the class Retailer. The class Retailer has two subclasses, Food-retailer and Mass-merchandiser.

Inheritance is used to define a hierarchy of classes going from the most general to the most specific classes of objects. In some systems, this hierarchy is called a *lattice*. You would define the most general classes with slots that should be present in all objects of this class. You would also define a general set of message handlers. In our system, there is a frame definition for Retailer. It holds everything common to both instances of Food-retailer and Mass-merchandiser. Behavior that is unique to Food-retailer, such as possessing a frozen foods section, is added to its class description using some combination of new slots and additional methods.

Many object-oriented programming languages and systems, including Goldworks, go far beyond the features described in this section. For instance, slots of classes can be defined with default values. Classes that inherit slots from other classes have the option of overriding the default values. Slots can possess other attributes besides a name and a value, including documentation text, constraints, and actions to be taken whenever the slot' s value is used or modified.

One of the strengths of object-oriented programming is the way it encourages the creation of an application with natural correspondence between the objects you manipulate in the implementation with those that are found in the real world. This is an especially strong argument in our case because the market model, like so many other models of behavior in business, is inherently object-based, providing descriptions of components, flows of money, goods, or information, and sequence of operations. An object-oriented approach makes it easier to document a system for the same reason.

Class Hierarchy

One of the most useful attributes of an object-oriented programming system or a frame-based system is the property of inheritance. Classes of objects (frames) can be defined in such a way that behavior from other classes is inherited. State variables and procedures can both be inherited. It is this feature from which most of the benefits of object-oriented programming arise.

Our system contains the following classes: brand manager's assistant, market, deal, retailer, items, brands, categories, and user interface. Note that most of the objects are natural counterparts in the world in which a brand manager works. Some objects are physical objects while others represent abstractions. There are some abstract objects, like retailer-response, that are not likely to be in a brand manager's vocabulary already.

The following sections describe the most important classes of objects in the system.

Brand Manager's Assistant

DEALMAKER can be thought of as an assistant to a brand manager. It helps the brand manager with one of his tasks. In implementing this system, we thought it would be useful to capture the notion of an assistant as a separate object. This object, an instance of the class brand-manager-assistant, is the agent controlling the program. It supports the basic sequence below by the messages it handles.

```
Pick a market and devise a plan.
View overall marketing plan.
Repeat.
```

Most interactions are accomplished by means of the brand manager's assistant. Understanding the behavior of this class of objects is the key to understanding the control flow of the prototype. It is the rough equivalent of the main program of conventional programs.

An instance of brand-manager-assistant holds many state variables in its slots. This was done in lieu of using global variables. The user interacts with the brand-manager-assistant using the commands on the menu bar and by using a mouse to push the other buttons visible on the screen. These actions are converted into messages to a brand-manager-assistant object. The brand manager assistant supports many messages, including Offer-deal, List-markets, and Explain-retailer-response.

Market Class

Objects representing markets resemble markets in the real world. There is no precise definition for the term, but usually *market* means some particular grouping of objects and institutions at some level. The term seems to be one of convenience, with its meaning dependent on the context. In this prototype, it has a precise definition. It is an object used to hold information about the retailers and consumers in a particular geographic location. We have objects for Chicago, Boston, and Los Angeles. Our definition of a market matches roughly what people mean when they refer to the market in city X.

Market objects are used to hold attributes of the area in which a set of retailers operate. We have slots for describing the following: the degree to which a market is sensitive to price changes versus features or displays, a list of the retailers in the area, and a list of the top brands in the market.

Deal

There is a frame in our system that defines a deal. It is a generalized representation of the objects that brand managers would think of as deals. There are slots in a deal frame for describing the relevant brand item, the discounts or allowances on price, advertising, and displays, and any additional conditions attached to a deal. There is also a slot to describe the markets at which this deal is targeted.

Retailer Class

The retailer class is the one for which we do the most specialization. We specialized so we could test assorted hypotheses we had about the proper use of rules and messages. Another reason to specialize would be to have different kinds of retailers; for instance, a food chain is a useful specialization of a retailer since there might be slots or rules that apply only to them. The class hierarchy for the retailer class is shown below.

```
Retailer
    Mass-merchandiser
    Food-retailer
            r1-retailer
            r2-retailer
            r3-retailer
```

The class *Retailer* is divided into two subclasses: *Mass-merchandiser* and *Food-retailer*. *Food-retailer* is split into two subclasses. Then at the lowest level are classes like *r1-retailer, r2-retailer*, etc. It is at this level that instances are created. The other levels are intended to be abstract classes used only to specify common characteristics of particular subclasses of retailers. Each of the low-level classes has only a single instance. This was done so that each could provide a separate method (handler) for the message *Respond-to-deal*. Having a separate method was the means to implement the different philosophies of the retailers. For example, one of the retailer objects in our system is an object named R1. It is an instance of R1-retailer. Its method for handling the Respond-to-deal message is a Lisp code that implements R1' s philosophy. The details of this message handler are described in the Discussion section later in this chapter.

Brand Items, Brands, Categories

These three classes of objects are extremely simple in this system. Only the obvious relationships are represented. That is, brand items belong to brands and brands are grouped into categories.

User Interface

The system is structured to separate the user interface from the rest of the system. This was done to allow us to plug in different user interfaces as they were developed. The interface that is visible in the present packaging of DEALMAKER makes use of the Screen Toolkit of Goldworks. It presents to the user a set of spreadsheet-like objects in which he can edit and view cell values.

Retailer Response to a Deal

As stated earlier, at the lowest level of the hierarchy for the retailer class are classes like *r1-retailer, r2-retailer*, etc. It is at this level that instances are created. The other levels are intended to be abstract classes used only to specify common characteristics of certain kinds of retailers. Each of the low level classes has only a single instance. This was done so that each could provide a separate method (handler) for the message *Respond-to-deal*. Having a separate method was the means to implement the different philosophies of the retailers.

The difference in implementation manifests itself in the handler for the message *Respond-to-deal*. The rule version of retailers has a handler that makes some preliminary assertions and then starts the backward-chaining process. The descriptions below illustrate the sequence of events for retailer R1. All retailers go through a similar process. Backward-chaining is initiated by attempting to satisfy the goal

```
(DEAL-CONSIDERED R1 A-DEAL)
```

In other words, the goal is to have R1 consider a deal. Consideration of a deal is broken up into several steps, as expressed by the rule below:

```
(define-rule R1-considers-a-deal
   (:direction :backward)
(retailer-accepts R1 ?deal ?yes-or-no)
```

```
(price-cut R1 ?deal ?p)
(display    R1 ?deal ?d)
(feature    R1 ?deal ?f)
(quantity  R1 ?deal ?q)
(retailer-reviewed-response R1)
THEN
(deal-considered R1 ?deal))
```

So the first step is to determine if the retailer will accept the deal. From there, values for price-cut, display, feature, and quantity are determined. The last step is a review process, which checks the results for consistency and makes the final decision with respect to the deal under consideration. Only then is the goal DEAL-CONSIDERED met.

To implement this, there is one separate set of rules for each subgoal. We found it useful to make use of a feature in Goldworks called goal-directed forward-chaining. Using that feature gives us the benefit of using a goal-directed search, a very natural way to think about the problem-solving process, and it also lets us make use of forward-chaining rules, which are very fast in Goldworks. To use it, you define a rule-set. A portion of one of R1's rule-sets is given below.

```
(DEFINE-RULE-SET retailer-R1-accepts-
    rule-set ()
    (retailer-accepts R1 ?deal ?yes-or-no)
    (DEFINE-RULE R1-considers-importance-
    of-brand ()
    ...
    THEN
    ...)
    ; ...more rules...
    )
```

A rule-set in Goldworks groups together forward-chaining rules and defines the context in which they are activated. The one above activates when an attempt is made to fulfill the goal

```
(retailer-accepts R1 ?deal ?yes-or-no)
```

There are similar rule-sets for each of the subgoals.

SAMPLE RULES FOR DETERMINING A RETAILER'S RESPONSE

In this section, we examine a few rules from DEALMAKER. This will show how we have captured knowledge about retailer behavior and give a brief introduction to rule programming in Goldworks. Consider the rule below.

```
(define-rule R1-considers-importance-of-brand ()
(deal-under-consideration R1 ?deal)
(current-market R1 ?market)
(instance ?deal is deal with brand-items ?item)
(instance ?item is brand-item with brand ?brand)
(brand-is-one-of-top-brands ?market ?brand 3)
THEN
(retailer-accepts R1 ?deal yes))
```

The translation of this Lisp-like notation into English would be something like

```
IF R1 is considering a deal in a market and
   the brand item is in the top three of its category
THEN R1 accepts the deal
```

A rule in Goldworks consists of one or more patterns in the IF part (the antecedent) and one or more patterns in the THEN part (the consequent). The patterns are matched against facts in the assertion base. When all of the patterns match assertions, the rule fires, adding assertions specified in the THEN part. Variables are used to indicate a pattern that can match more than one assertion. Variables begin with a question mark (?). Variables are bound to values when they match an assertion. For example, the first pattern

```
(deal-under-consideration R1 ?deal)
```

matches the following assertion

```
(deal-under-consideration R1 a-deal)
```

For the rest of the rule, the variable ?deal has a value of (is bound to) the instance A-DEAL. Variables are used in almost all rules because it was necessary to create a fairly complex environment to do what we wanted for DEALMAKER. There are many instances of retailers, many instances of markets, many instances of brands, etc. Variables are the means with which to cope with multiple instances.

The rule above is the one that captures the essence of R1's policy for deals. As you recall, R1 always accepts a deal for a brand as long as that brand is in the top three brands in its category. The first pattern defines the context in which the rule should apply. It states that the first condition for using this rule is that we're in the process of having R1 consider a deal. The last pattern in the IF part expresses the requirement that the brand is one of the top three. The middle three patterns are setting up variables for use in the last pattern. The assertion matching the pattern

```
(current-market R1 ?market)
```

tells us the market being considered. Remember that retailers do business in more than one market. The assertions matching

```
(instance ?deal is deal with brand-item ?item)
(instance ?item is brand-item with brand ?brand)
```

tell us the brand item the deal pertains to and determines its brand. So then we have values for ?market and ?brand for use in the final pattern

```
(brand-is-one-of-top-brands ?market ?brand 3)
```

If all of these patterns match, the assertions given in the consequent of the rule are added to the assertion base. If we are working on A-DEAL, that means the assertion

```
(retailer-accepts R1 a-deal yes)
```

would be added.

Note that the original rule looks very much like Lisp code. Goldworks is an expert system toolkit built on top of a Lisp system and sometimes the Lisp base shows through.

SOLUTION USING RETRACTION

We had several different retailers to implement for this system, each with a different philosophy. While implementing these different philosophies, we also explored different ways to use rules to obtain a solution. The preceding section described one of the rules used to determine if R1 accepts a deal. It is a fairly straightforward use of rules. In this section, we describe a more unconventional use of rules.

In many AI systems, having a truth maintenance subsystem has been very useful. *Truth maintenance* is a term that originated at MIT in the work of Jon Doyle.[3] To choose actions, reasoning systems must be able to make assumptions and subsequently revise their beliefs when discoveries contradict these assumptions. The truth maintenance system is a problem solver subsystem for performing these functions of recording and maintaining the reasons for program belief. Basically, what a truth maintenance system is providing is a way to make assumptions about the world, to reach conclusions based on those assumptions, and then to be able to keep the set of conclusions consistent with the set of assumptions even as the assumptions change.

In Goldworks, truth maintenance manifests itself in the way in which assertions are managed. Any fact in the assertion base can be removed. This leads to the deletion of all logically dependent assertions, that is, the ones that were added as rules fired because of the original assertion(s). They refer to the deletion of an assertion as *retraction*.

We made use of retraction of assertions in providing a solution to the problem of determining a retailer's response to a deal. It helped us select a solution given a set of possible answers. Assume you have a problem that you solve by choosing a value for a variable. Suppose that you know all the values that the variable in question can assume. A typical AI solution involves combining this information with a set of tests or constraints that you can apply to each of the possible values. Acceptable solutions to the problem must come from the set of possible values and must pass all the tests. To get a solution, you apply all of the test functions repeatedly, removing any possible solutions that fail tests, and stopping when all remaining acceptable answers pass all the tests. At that point you have converted your set of all possible answers to the set of acceptable answers.

This method of solution can be implemented quite well in Goldworks. You start by assuming that all possible answers are acceptable so you make an assertion for each one. For example, if you know that promotion price is always chosen from the set of price points {0.89 0.99 1.09 1.19 1.29}, you add an assertion to Goldworks' assertion base of the form (PROMOTION-PRICE ?P). In effect, you are assuming that all possible answers are true. The assertion base would have all of the assertions following.

```
(promotion-price 0.89)
(promotion-price 0.99)
(promotion-price 1.09)
(promotion-price 1.19)
(promotion-price 1.29)
```

Then using the inference engine, you fire rules that test whether a promotion price is acceptable. If you find an unacceptable one, remove the assertion by retraction. Keep going until no more rules fire, at which time you have zero or more PROMOTION-PRICE assertions remaining. Assuming your rules are correct and complete, any one of these remaining assertions is an acceptable solution. For instance, you might have the following in the assertion base when all rules have fired.

```
(promotion-price 1.09)
(promotion-price 1.19)
```

Note how this method reinforces the notion of knowledge as independent chunks that you can add to your knowledge base. The following rule set illustrates this method.

```
(DEFINE-RULE-SET retailer-R1-price-cut-rule-set ()
(price-cut R1 ?deal ?p)

(define-rule R1-does-not-cut-price (:priority -500)
(true)
THEN
(price-cut R1 ?deal 0))

(define-rule R1-determines-price-cut ()
(promotion-price ?promo-price)
(regular-price    ?regular-price)
THEN
(price-cut R1 ?deal
(evaluate (regular-price-price-cut ?regular-price
?promo-price)))
AND-THEN
(promotion-price R1 ?deal ?promo-price))

(define-rule R1-rejects-promotion-price-if-less-than-mfg-price ()
(promotion-price ?p)            -> ?promo
(manufacturer-price ?deal ?mp)
(< ?p ?mp)
THEN
(rejected-price ?p)
AND-THEN (retract ?promo))

(define-rule R1-rejects-promotion-price-if-margin-test-fails ()
(promotion-price ?p)            -> ?promo
(manufacturer-price ?deal ?mp)
(margin-target ?margin)
```

```
(price-does-not-meet-margin-target ?p ?mp ?margin)
THEN
(rejected-price ?p)
AND-THEN (retract ?promo))
; ...more rules...
); end rule-set
```

The second line defines the goal pattern for this rule-set. This set of forward chaining rules is activated whenever a attempt is made to satisfy the goal

```
(price-cut R1 ?deal ?p)
```

In other words, when we want to know what price-cut a retailer puts into effect in response to a deal, this set of rules is activated.

The rest of the body of the rule-set defines the forward-chaining rules that can add an assertion satisfying the goal pattern to the assertion base. The first rule defined, R1-DOES-NOT-CUT-PRICE, is a low priority rule, which means it fires only after every other rule has had a chance to fire. It is present to ensure that the goal is always attained. It is saying, "If you can' t decide anything, don' t cut the price." The rule R1-DETERMINES-PRICE-CUT says that you can determine the value for price-cut only after you know the regular price and the promotion price. The priority of that rule is slightly lower than other rules: –1 versus 0. That is to allow our method of solution – keep testing possible answers until no more rules fire – to remove all unacceptable answers before we choose from the acceptable answers. The next two rules are chunks of knowledge that say when to reject a suggested promotion price. The first says that R1 never wants to promote an item if it means R1 will take a loss on the item. The second says that R1 must meet a specific margin target with any promotion price.

CONSUMER BEHAVIOR MODEL

The models we use in this system relate the consumer demand to measures of price cut (P), feature (F), and display (D). Models are of the form

$$\text{Units} = c_0 + c_1{}^*P + c_2{}^*F + c_3{}^*D$$

Internally, these models are represented as a structured data object in Lisp. A function is provided to compute the value of units associated with a combination of P, D, and F values. Its use is illustrated below.

```
(predicted-units :price-cut 0.10 :feature 10)
```

The fact that the description of consumer behavior models is so short highlights the difference between representing knowledge numerically and representing it symbolically.

CONCLUSIONS AND POSSIBILITIES FOR FUTURE WORK

DEALMAKER has been described as an expandable system. That is, by the addition of other components to the model, other instances of the present set of market elements or rule-sets with objectives other than those implemented to date, the reusable components of this application could be applied in the development of other prototypes. The system could be extended or its nature could be changed.

Making Extensions to DEALMAKER

DEALMAKER was implemented in a modular fashion. Right from the start, consideration was given on how to build on top of DEALMAKER. Part of this is a consequence of using an object-oriented approach to the design. The end result is that there are at least two simple ways to extend the work we have done on DEALMAKER. One is to extend it by adding knowledge in the form of rule-sets. The other is to extend it by adding new classes of objects that are specializations of existing classes.

Extensions by Rule-sets

A rule-set for determining a retailer's response to a deal is a plug-compatible module. By that we mean that it has a very well defined interface to the rest of the system. As long as you match that interface, you can replace existing rule-sets or you can add additional retailers.

In all rule-base retailers, the handler for the message Respond-to-deal initiates backward-chaining by attempting to satisfy the goal

```
(DEAL-CONSIDERED ?RETAILER ?DEAL)
```

where ?RETAILER would be the name of the retailer who is supposed to consider the deal. All you need to do is define a backward-chaining set of rules that satisfies that goal pattern. You can do this in Goldworks using either backward-chaining rules or goal-directed forward-chaining using rule-sets.

There is another level at which you may plug in your own set of rules. As you recall, each of the rule-based implementations of retailers have a backward-chaining rule that looks like

```
(define-rule R1-considers-a-deal (:direction :backward)
(retailer-accepts R1 ?deal ?yes-or-no)
(price-cut R1 ?deal ?p)
(display   R1 ?deal ?d)
(feature   R1 ?deal ?f)
(quantity  R1 ?deal ?q)
(retailer-reviewed-response R1)
THEN
(deal-considered R1 ?deal))
```

This presents six additional possibilities for plugging in your own knowledge. For example, if you wanted to derive the size of the price cut using a different method, you could define a set of rules that satisfied the goal

```
(price-cut R1 ?deal ?price-cut)
```

The current implementation defines a rule-set for each of these subgoals of the process of determining a retailer response.

Extensions by Specialization

Another way to extend DEALMAKER is to take advantage of its object-oriented framework. We have defined many different classes of objects. There are frames for markets, retailers, deals, responses, etc. Any of these are candidates for specialization.

For example, we broke the class retailer into two kinds of retailers: food retailers and mass merchandiser. Even though the current system does not make use of any mass merchandisers, having a separate class illustrates the point. Having separate classes and the ability to define behavior that is unique to that class are very easy to do in an object-based system.

CHANGING THE NATURE OF DEALMAKER

The following are possible changes in the nature and purpose of DEALMAKER.

From Simulator to Educator

The current system is a simulator since it allows you to explore the consequences of actions you might take. One possible way to extend it would be to enhance the explanation capabilities of the system to go beyond simply explaining why certain results occurred. It might be very useful to have a system that could explain the underlying market model, where it works best, and where it doesn' t. To the extent that the system accurately reflects the manufacturer and the retailers it does business with, this system could serve as a training vehicle for people trying to learn marketing or trying to learn the company.

From Simulator to Mentor

Another possibility is to shift the role of the system toward the role often played by a person' s manager: a mentor. This system would offer to review your work and offer suggestions on places to look at more closely or reminders to consider alternate viewpoints.

From Simulator to Monitoring System

There is no real representation of time in the current system. Simulated events happen at some unspecified time in the future. Representing time is one area in which the current system could be extended. Beyond that it might also be useful to begin comparing the expected outcome to the actual outcome. This kind of system should be able to do the comparison and explain the difference, perhaps by finding invalid assumptions.

NOTES

1. Kunz, John C., Thomas P. Kehler, and Michael D. Williams. "Applications Development Using a Hybrid AI Development System," *The AI Magazine*, Fall, 1984, pp. 41-54.

2. Stefik, Mark, and Daniel G. Bobrow. "Object-Oriented Programming: Themes and Variations," *The AI Magazine*, Winter 1986, pp. 40-62.

3. Doyle, Jon. "A Truth Maintenance System," *Artificial Intelligence*, Vol. 12, 1979, pp. 231-273.

CHAPTER 12

RELATED RESEARCH

The first eleven chapters presented research conducted in the Marketing Workbench Laboratory. There have been other related research efforts that have produced important results. This chapter provides an overview of this research, concentrating on papers in the same vein as the lab' s research.

THREE ANALYSIS SYSTEMS

This section contains a description of three expert system prototypes that analyze scanner data.

Share Analysis Expert System (SHANEX)

Alpar[1] developed an expert system for doing share analysis in a manner similar to a brand manager. Interviews with brand managers indicated that they analyzed the level and trend in market share, and changes in share were traced to changes in retail trade support and price. The result was a series of qualitative statements about the underlying quantitative data. This report was produced by share analysts who apply a systematic process:

They look through the data to locate a change in market share.

When such a change is located, they look to see if any causal factors were present during the time periods of the share change.

If the causal factors are present, they make a statement about the share change and attribute it to the causal factors.

They continue in this manner until all share changes have been located and analyzed.

SHANEX captures this process in about 160 rules in a PROLOG program running on a personal computer. These rules play various roles, for instance determining if one of the brand's attributes has changed. The following is an example of such a SHANEX rule:

```
if attribute is price and
    attribute is expressed as an index and
    attribute value is X and
    X is greater than 106
then the attribute has moved up.
```

This rule sets the conditions under which a change in price should be considered significant enough to attempt to relate it to changes in market share. Attributes include variables in the database such as share, price, display, and advertising. The following is one of SHANEX's rules that performs this type of relational logic:

```
if a unit's market share was not stable and
    trade support moved in the same direction and
    price moved in the same direction
then (A) "market share was affected by trade support despite price"
    and
      (B) consider "market share was affected by trade support" for
          overall pattern.
```

This rule represents the core of SHANEX's analysis: It contains knowledge about the direction that the attribute pairs should move. Share and trade support should move in the same direction; if trade support is up, then share should be up. Share and price should move in the opposite direction; if price is up, then share should be down. This particular rule recognizes that the effect of one attribute (trade support) on share may be stronger than the effect of another attribute (price).

These types of rules can examine a brand's share relationships in various units, where a unit is an area of the country or an individual retail account. The (B) part of the above rule involves the process of aggregating or generalizing the relationships found for individual units into an overall pattern. Another set of rules searches for patterns in these statements, and thus produces a higher-order analysis.

These rules produce a report with statements like the following ones:

```
Market share analysis:
Nela total share was high (42.5%).
Nela powder share was high (32%).
Nela liquid share was average (10.5%).
```

These statements about individual forms and sizes of the Nela brand are then generalized:

```
Nela total share was up due to powder up despite liquid stable.
```

Causal statements are also generated:

```
Nela powder 32 oz.: Market share was up, mainly affected by trade support.
In CM share was up due to trade support despite price up.
```

SHANEX represents an innovative approach to expert systems in marketing, which is similar to an Era III system because it is based upon an underlying causal model that relates market share to two causal factors: price and trade support. This causal model is not a quantitative one but a qualitative model which can be described as a *direction of causality* model: the model contains knowledge of the direction or sign of the relationship between share and the causal factors. The following is a succinct statement of the model:

```
Causal factor        Sign
trade support         +
price                 —
```

SHANEX shows that this very simple model can produce results that mirror those of a share analyst, thus saving firms many hours of labor.

SCAN*EXPERT

Bayer and Harter[2] have developed SCAN*EXPERT for assisting users of A. C. Nielsen's scanner data by searching through scanner data to determine a brand's key competitors, locate events that might be of interest, and then search for the causes of these events. The system contains knowledge about phenomena which a manager might find interesting, and knows how to propose and test hypotheses about the causes of these phenomena.

SCAN*EXPERT contains two distinct types of knowledge: 1) knowledge about the processes of analyzing marketing data, and 2) knowledge about how to perform a specific analysis. The overall goal of the analysis is similar to SHANEX's: locate changes in market share and explain why they occurred. A unique contribution of Bayer and Harter's research is the knowledge engineering of a group of Nielsen client service representatives who regularly perform this type of share analysis. These interviews were primarily concerned with the first task of identifying the process of analyzing marketing data. The research led to the conclusion that the analysts tended to use one of three stylized modes of search through the data: Miner, Manager, or Researcher.

The Miner mines the data using a data driven strategy in which interesting events are located by searching through the data and then explanations are sought from the data. Because the database is so huge, the Miner employs a directed approach in which known causes of events are evaluated in a hierarchical manner. Bayer and Harter use rules like the following to propose hypotheses for interesting events:

```
if there is a increase in market share for a brand_size
then this is caused by a corresponding increase in retailer
     displays and corresponding increase in retailer major ads
     and decrease in retail price for the brand_size.
```

This is another example of a *direction of causality* model being applied to the analysis of scanner data.

The Manager has a priori knowledge that a particular issue is important and has knowledge about how to use the data to explore the issue. This expert system has knowledge that allows it to postulate reasons for the issue and to then test the hypotheses in a hierarchical manner. These issues seem to be posed as questions of the type, What are the trends for the product in this particular market? These questions require deeper knowledge to answer than the types of knowledge used by Miner.

The Researcher looks for known types of marketing opportunities: new products, packages, or ways of doing business. Bayer and Harter present an example of the Researcher knowing that a niche strategy may be a good approach. It searches for a profitable niche player, determines how this niche player is doing business, and then generates hypotheses about the way the user's business could alternatively be done.

INFER

Harlam, Lodish, and Rangaswamy[3] developed the INFER system to attack the same problem as the first two systems: automatic data analysis that identifies problems and generates a report. The first version of INFER has two goals: 1) to produce statements about what is happening in the market and 2) to interpret the data to explain why events are occurring. INFER is based upon interviews with potential users of the INFOSCAN database from Information Resources, Inc., and the authors' own knowledge of data analysis and interpretation.

The following data are available for analysis: volume sales, dollar sales, volume share, dollar share, average regular price, average percent price reduction, percent all commodity volume (ACV) with display only, percent ACV with feature only, and percent ACV with feature and display. These variables are used to explain what was happening to items of a product category that are aggregated in various ways: by brand, subcategory, manufacturer, geographical area, time period, or the total category.

INFER generates a set of statistics and measures before the data analysis begins. It contains algorithms for calculating various statistics such as means and standard deviations, and an innovative measure of volatility to detect large period-to-period fluctuations in a time series. This expert system combines the concepts from Era II and III systems: a regression model is run for each brand' s volume using data on the available causal factors. Correlations between all pairs of brand volumes are computed and stored. These statistics are generated in the EXPRESS system and the output is sent to a file that can be read by M.1, the expert system shell containing INFER' s rules. After analytical results have been obtained about various levels of the product category, rules exist for converting these results into English language statements for inclusion in a report.

Related Work Outside Marketing

All three systems share an important characteristic: They contain rules about how to perform an analysis in addition to rules about the way to perform a particular analysis. This is necessary with knowledge-based systems because they do not contain common sense or general knowledge, which humans can use to guide an analysis. SCAN*EXPERT is unique among the three because it was based upon an extensive knowledge engineering exercise that generated three separate analytical strategies.

There has been related work in this area by people who are examining the types of computer environments needed to support data analysis by humans. Tukey[4] challenged statisticians to pay attention to the issues involved in managing an analysis process. This challenge seems to have led others[5] to develop systems for managing the data analysis process. Lubinsky and Pregibon[6] present a formalization of the space of descriptions used by data analysts and describe heuristics for searching through this space. They implemented TESS, a Tree-based Environment for developing Statistical Strategy and applied it to the problem of fitting regression equations. This line of research is increasing the awareness among statisticians and computer scientists of the need to monitor and record an expert analyst' s processes. These efforts will lead to additional research into the processes used by such experts.

This nonmarketing research can be useful in the future developments of marketing systems. But, the types of systems described above and discussed in the earlier parts of this book are fundamentally different from these approaches. Marketing-related systems contain both analysis knowledge and marketing knowledge, while the general systems have to be domain independent. But all of this work shares one common theme: Knowledge-based systems require both process and analysis knowledge.

ANALOGICAL REASONING

Bayer and Harter's model of a Researcher introduces the notion of locating one pattern in the data and then using it to search for other matching situations. This is a type of reasoning by analogy in which the idea is to find situations that are analogous to a target situation. The analogical problem-solving approach has been part of the AI tool kit for several years[7] and recently applied by Burke[8] to the marketing domain. Burke argues that the knowledge engineering approach which is normally used for the development of an expert system, is difficult to apply in marketing because most of our knowledge is in the form of empirical research rather than in well-accepted heuristics or theories. When he examines the empirical research, he finds that the relationships found in the research depend critically on the research context. When these research results are used as the foundation for an expert system, the dependencies that are context sensitive must be explicitly recognized in the rule premises. This problem seems to arise because of the lack of generalizability of most marketing studies and experiments.

Burke proposes an alternative approach: Represent the empirical knowledge in its original context and extract the knowledge when it is needed. His approach is to dynamically abstract the empirical knowledge to analogous new situations. This approach is illustrated with ADDUCE, a frame-based system for reasoning about consumer response to advertising. ADDUCE predicts how consumers will react to a new ad by searching for relevant advertising studies and then generalizing the results to the new ad. This generalization is based upon the matching of the new ad's context with the context of the original experiments by the analogical reasoning process that Burke succinctly describes:

> Analogical reasoning consists of transferring knowledge from past experimental contexts to new situations that share significant aspects, and then using the transferred knowledge to predict outcomes in the new situations.[9]

ADDUCE is a Prolog program that predicts how consumers will react to a new ad, based upon descriptions of the ad, the audience, and the market. The basic idea is to describe each of these three characteristics as multi-attribute objects. For instance, magazine ads are an object with the following attributes and possible attribute values:

- arguments (strong, weak)
- exposure (forced, nonforced)

- featured brand
- presenter identify (celebrity, person on the street)

Such information about the objects are encoded in a frame-based representation. Frames are an AI concept for organizing information about objects and specifying the processes of making inferences about and among the objects. Each attribute is a slot in a frame, and a slot can perform various functions: 1) store the value of the attribute, 2) know how to retrieve a default value if none is available, 3) contain a procedure for obtaining a value for the attribute when one is needed by the inference engine.

Relationships among objects are represented using Prolog rules. The following is an English language version of a typical rule, which was developed from an experiment reported by Petty, Cacioppo, and Schumann:[10]

```
if subjects are pcs83-subjects and
    audience involvement is low and
    communication to the audience is via an ad and
    presenter is identified as a celebrity
then attitude = positive.
```

ADDUCE first obtains a description of the new ad in terms of its three characteristics: ad, audience, and market. It then calculates a similarity measure between this new object and all objects known to the system. The measure of similarity is the number of characteristics shared by the two objects minus the number of distinctive characteristics of the two objects. The next step is to use the similarity measure to locate similar objects. Finally, the knowledge contained in the similar objects are used to make predictions about the new object.

Analogical reasoning could play a major role in marketing information systems because it provides a mechanism for bringing past knowledge to bear on new situations. For instance, important knowledge involves marketing events that occurred for all the items in a product category. These events could be described in terms of several characteristics: brand, event type, market, time period, etc. If all past marketing events were encoded in a common frame representation, then a system could be developed that comments on a manager' s plan. If the plan were developed on the computer in an Era IV type system, then the computer could treat the events in the plan as objects. It would search for similar events and then use the performance of those events to predict the performance of each element of the new plan.

AN ERA IV SYSTEM

Era IV systems support marketing planning and design, and thus contain marketing knowledge rather than analysis knowledge. ADCAD is an expert system developed by Burke, et al.[11] which assists in the design of an advertising strategy. It assists managers with the formulation of advertising objectives, copy strategy, and the selection of communication approaches. This assistance is obtained by using expert system technology to help advertising to use and apply insights from published research and practitioner experience.

In the traditional AI literature, designing something is usually considered to be a configuration problem in which the designer is specifying the values of a number of attributes of the object being designed. When treated in this way, forward-chaining expert systems have been the dominant approach to building design or planning systems. Burke deviates from this approach and make use of M.1 to implement a backward chaining rule-based system. This decision seems to have flowed from a study of the problem domain, which indicated that the ad design problem could be decomposed into a series of linked selection problems: select product benefits, the format, presenter, and executional techniques, and the emotional tone of the advertisement. Each of these selections is made from a relatively short list of potential solutions, thus making backward-chaining a suitable approach to the ad design application.

ADCAD' s knowledge base was obtained from empirical advertising studies, theories of advertising effectiveness, heuristics obtained in advertising textbooks and trade magazines, and creative staff in a major advertising agency. The knowledge engineering process that generated this knowledge base appears to be the most extensive to date. The result is an impressive capture and codification of the advertising literature into a form that a standard expert system inference engine can use to provide advice about an important marketing problem: advertising design.

NOTES

1. Alpar, Paul. "Knowledge-Based Modeling of Marketing Managers' Problem Solving Behavior," Working Paper M/C 294, College of Business, The University of Illinois at Chicago. The rules and examples in this section were taken from this working paper.

2. Bayer, Judy, and Rachel Harter. " ' Miner,' ' Manager,' and ' Researcher' : Three Expert Modes of Analysis of Scanner Data," Working Paper, Carnegie Mellon University, February 1989.

3. Harlam, Bari, Leonard M. Lodish, and Arvind Rangaswamy. "INFER: An Expert System for Automatic Analysis of Scanner Data," Working Paper, The Wharton School, University of Pennsylvania, February 1989.

4. Tukey, J. W. "Another Look at the Future," in *Computer Science and Statistics: Proceedings of the 14th Symposium on the Interface*, Troy, New York: Springer-Verlag, 1983, pp. 2-8.

5. Carr, Daniel B., Paula J. Cowley, M. A. Whiting, and Wesley L. Nicholson. "Organizational Tools for Data Analysis Environments," in Proceedings of the Statistical Computing Section, American Statistical Association, 1984, pp. 214-218.

6. Lubinsky, David, and Daryl Pregibon. "Data Analysis as Search," Journal of Econometrics, Volume 38, No. 1/2, May/June 1988, pp. 247-268.

7. Carbonell, Jaime G. "A Computational Model of Analogical Problem Solving", *Proceedings of the Seventh International Joint Conference on Artificial Intelligence*, Palo Alto, CA: Morgan Kaufmann Publishers, 1981.

8. Burke, Raymond R. "Reasoning with Knowledge in Context," Working Paper, The Wharton School, University of Pennsylvania, March 1989.

9. Burke, op. cit., p. 4.

10. Petty, Richard E., John T. Cacioppo, and David Schumann. "Central and Peripheral Routes to Advertising Effectiveness: The Moderating Role of Involvement," *Journal of Consumer Research*, Vol. 10, September 1983, pp. 135-146.

11. Burke, Raymond R., Arvind Rangaswamy, Jerry Wind, and Jehoshua Eliashberg. "ADCAD: A Knowledge-based System for Advertising Design," Working Paper, The Wharton School, University of Pennsylvania, December 1988.

CHAPTER 13

IMPLEMENTATION ISSUES

The preceding chapters have provided the reader with an understanding of

1) the impact scanner data are having on marketing and marketing systems and the potential role of expert systems (chapter 1),
2) the probable evolutionary path (the Eras of Marketing Systems) that is required for marketing systems in this changing world (chapter 2),
3) the basic technologies that underlie **existing** expert system applications that deal with this impact (section II and chapters 7 and 11 in section III),
4) the types of applications that one must build in each era (section III).

This is clearly an important area, as witnessed by the financial commitment of the firms who have sponsored the research in the various universities. Almost all of the research reported in this book has been conducted with some degree of cooperation of consumer goods firms.

The research at Duke's Marketing Workbench Laboratory has been followed very closely by most of the consumer goods firms. Over 20 such firms have been formal sponsors of the laboratory. This sponsorship allows the firms to attend quarterly meetings and to receive copies of all the systems developed in the lab. In addition, day-long programs have been held at Duke, which have been attended by senior managers from almost all consumer packaged goods firms.

Since these firms are not required to report on how they use the prototypes, very little structured information is available about the implementation of the systems. There has been a growing awareness among businesses that information and information technology can provide a strategic, competitive advantage. This awareness has led to a reluctance by firms to discuss their computing strategies and their critical systems. This situation is accentuated with expert systems. If a firm believes that it can gain an advantage from such systems, it is not eager to inform its competitors of the existence and nature of its expert systems. The result is reluctance by most firms to provide the details of their expert system efforts.

However, it has been possible to identify three groups of firms by how they have responded to the prototypes described in this book: System Implementors, Conceptual Implementors, and Watchers.

System Implementors

A system implementor is a firm that implements one or more of the prototype systems developed in a research setting. Such implementation can take two forms: 1) a separate expert system, or 2) a new component of the existing MMIS. This section describes one instance of a nearly complete implementation of the prototypes developed in the Marketing Workbench Laboratory, and several implementations of one or more of the prototypes.

Firm A: This firm reported that it had built an expert system that implemented all four eras, and that the implementation followed the prototypes described in this book. The firm worked with a vendor of a PC-based statistical package to build a extended version of the coupled system.

A manager would apply the system by using a menu system to specify the brand and market to be analyzed. The expert system then log-on to the firm's MMIS and extracts the appropriate data for the brand and market. It then sends the data to the statistical package and instructs the package to build a model. After a satisfactory model has been developed, the expert system asks the user if s/he wants to view the model results. If so, the system goes through a graphical presentation very similar to the one in the Model Animation prototype. Finally, the system asks the user if s/he wants to plan a marketing event. If so, a scaled-down version of DEALMAKER is brought into play. The manager can specify values of price, display, and feature, and the system uses the model to ascertain the probable impact of these causal factor levels on brand performance in the market.

The developer reports that the system was introduced to marketing managers in a live application. A marketing manager came to the MIS group with a problem that could not be handled by the current information systems. After listening to the marketing manager describe the problem, the development manager turned on the expert system and went through a live session with the marketing manager. In the course of an hour, the manager had gained insight into the forces that were causing the brand's problem and had arrived at a solution. This manager spread the word about the new system among other marketing managers, and thus prepared the ground for the formal introduction of the system.

The development manager reports that this initial effort has grown significantly, and that related expert systems are being implemented throughout the firm's marketing and sales organizations.

Firm B: This firm did not adopt an expert system shell. Instead, a marketing research manager converted the Era II and III prototypes into the language of the firm' s MMIS. The following is a loose transcription of this manager' s description of his efforts:

> *I took the ideas in the Marketmetrics Knowledge System and implemented them in our Metaphor system. I set up a routine which runs a regression which relates a brand' s market share with its causal factors (price, display, and ad feature). This routine loops through all of our markets, and outputs a regression result for each market. I have another routine which takes this regression output and classifies the market into different groups. If the R-square value is below a cut-off, the routine reports that the brand does not respond to the causal factors in that market. If the market passes this R-square test, it then looks at the T-statistics for each of the causal factors. If they are all significant, the routine reports that the brand responds to all the causal factors in the market. Otherwise, it looks to see which causal factors are significant and classifies the market accordingly. A final routine summarizes these results for each market so that a marketing or sales manager can understand which factors influence which brands in which markets.*

Firm C: This firm built a system that operated similarly to Firm B' s. It was programmed in the BASIC programming language provided in the Metaphor system. It was different from Firm B' s because it was programmed to use the models to identify abnormal situations. The result was an exception report for each brand.

Firm D: A somewhat similar system was built by this firm in its Express system. It used rules to process data about a market, with a goal of writing a short memo to a regional sales manager that identified those brands and retail accounts not performing up to the national level.

Firm E: Another firm had a need to do sophisticated modeling of all the items in a product category, and to apply this model to a large number of categories. The initial efforts of the researchers in this company was on the development of Fortran programs for use by an analyst in building the models. After examining the concepts involved in the Marketmetrics Knowledge System, the manager decided to build marketmetric rules into the Fortran programs so that the system would be much smarter. This decision was based upon two factors: 1) the job was too big for expensive analysts to undertake using traditional statistical software, and 2) the Marketmetrics Knowledge System demonstrated that it was possible to apply marketmetrics knowledge via rules.

After several months in development, the manager reported that the system contained about 100 rules and could do about 90% of the work involved in building the models. After another three months, the manager reported that he was into "rule spaghetti" – there were so many rules that the Fortran language was proving to be suboptimal for the development of such a system. He now saw the advantage of a coupled systems approach.

Firm F: This firm had created a large number of regional marketing managers and given them responsibility for designing and implementing marketing programs in their regions. This firm implemented a version of the Baby Promotion Advisor as a means of assisting the regional marketing managers in their promotion planning. These manager had sales experience, but did not have the requisite knowledge for designing promotions. The firm reported that the system was deployed in the regional offices and used by the managers.

It appears that the system was primarily used as a way to educate the managers about promotion planning. The manager would describe a situation to the system and then use the expert system's explanation ability to understand how the system arrived at its advice. Repeated application of this process allowed the managers to become knowledgeable about promotion design. The system was no longer needed by these managers. However, it continued to be used as part of the training process for new regional marketing managers.

Conceptual Implementors

The material presented in this book has been important in the planning by some firms, even though these firms have not yet implemented expert systems. As the title implies, firms will need to evolve from pure information systems to knowledge systems. Conceptual Implementors devise a plan for this evolution, continue to study the expert system technologies and methodologies, and implement their information systems with an eye towards the evolution to knowledge systems. These firms report that they have been strongly influenced by the idea that they must evolve from a How's Business? system to a What's Driving My Business? system. They also report that the material in this book has provided them with a conceptual framework for this evolution.

Watchers

A Watcher is a firm that is watching or monitoring the expert systems efforts in university laboratories, but does not have a plan for implementing expert systems. Watchers fall into two classes: firms with, and firms without, a successful MMIS.

The Watcher firms with a successful MMIS are so successful that their marketing and sales managers do not see the need for the types of expert systems described in this book. These firms tend to practice national marketing, and thus do not have to do extensive analysis and planning at the local level. The Watcher firms without a success MMIS are too involved with the planning of such a system to have the time for expert systems. Their attitude seems to be one of monitoring the expert system world so that they will be in a position to make the transition to knowledge systems once their MMIS platforms are in place.

IMPLEMENTATION IMPEDIMENTS

This section describes several impediments to the implementation of expert systems in consumer goods firms.

Time. Expert systems take time to develop, just as all computer programs. However, with most traditional systems, almost all of the development time is spent by information systems professionals. But marketing-oriented expert systems require significant amounts of the marketing expert' s time. If that expert is a marketing manager, then the allocation of the necessary time is a major problem.

The experiences of one firm highlights this implementation impediment. The MIS managers in the firm reported that they delayed their sponsorship of the Marketing Workbench Laboratory until they had identified an appropriate expert system application, obtained the necessary funding, and gained the cooperation of a marketing manager who would serve as the expert. When the IS managers attended their first Marketing Workbench meeting, they were very excited about the application and eager to get started. Three months later, the MIS managers reported that the project was in jeopardy because the marketing manager had not been able to find the time for the project. After another three months, they indicated that the project had been canceled due to this time problem; the marketing manager was simply too busy doing marketing to spend the time in the knowledge engineering process.

This experience has been true for other firms, and points to the problem of getting managers to sit still long enough for the appropriate knowledge engineering.

Lack of expertise. Marketing is not viewed as a science by most marketing managers, and these managers do not have a clear way to distinguish one marketing expert from another. This became evident in attempting to implement the Baby Promotion Advisor in a sponsoring company. The first task was to identify the marketing managers in the firm who knew the most about promotion design. Key informants were asked to provide the identification. Time and again, these people identified marketing managers who had been successful in introducing a new brand or in building volume for an established brand. Further probing indicated that these respondents felt that these managers must be the most knowledgeable about promotion design because they had achieved the most success as a brand or marketing manager. Subsequent interviews with the managers indicated that they lacked a systematic approach to promotion planning and were not likely to be good sources for the expert system. These interviews further confirmed the existence of the time impediment.

This early experience was confirmed in subsequent interactions with managers in other firms. Most successful marketing managers are generalists, and if the firm does not explicitly collect and organize its knowledge, then marketing knowledge tends to be diffused throughout the organization. Managers are not rewarded for being experts on individual elements of the marketing mix; they are rewarded for putting together innovative marketing mixes that work in the market place. Such managers make use of expertise wherever they find it, and seem to meld individual knowledge chunks into a cohesive plan.

" I do not think Jack is better than me." There is a reluctance on the part of one marketing manager to recognize that another one is significantly better than s/he. This means that an expert system that contains Jack' s marketing expertise may not be accepted by Jill. Even if Jill does believe that Jack is a slightly better marketer, she may be reluctant to make use of the expert system that contains Jack' s knowledge. If she does make such use and the project is a success, who will get the credit? Jill, or Jack via his expert system? Taking one marketing manager' s expertise, in the form of an expert system, to another marketing manager is similar to the old concept of taking coals to Newcastle. Just as people in a coal-rich area do not need to import coal, it is not at all clear that one marketing manager needs to use the knowledge of another.

An expert system is a model. An expert system is an abstraction of expertise in a form that allows a computer to reason with the model. Hence, an expert system is a model, and models have a long history of being difficult to implement. Managers distrust the idea of trusting my business to a model. Hence they tend to distrust the idea of basing their decisions on the advice of a computer program.

I rent my knowledge to this firm; why should I put it into an expert system? A manager is paid to apply his or her knowledge for the benefit of the firm. This does not involve selling that knowledge to the firm; it involves renting the knowledge for the duration of employment. When the manager leaves the firm, the knowledge leaves with him or her. But if the manager puts the knowledge into a computer, the traditional employee/employer relationship has been broken. Without sufficient rewards for such knowledge computerization, the managers do not have an incentive to cooperate in the expert system process. Two firms have reported that they have overcome this problem by using retired managers as their source of expertise. These retired managers receive payment for selling their expertise to the firm where they had been employed.

It will expose what I do and do not know. Knowledge engineering results in a public display of the knowledge that an expert has been keeping hidden for years. Although this expert may routinely apply his or her knowledge for the benefit of the firm, s/he does not usually have to state all that s/he knows about a subject. The construction of an expert systems requires that the expert reveal what s/he does and does not know. Such revelation can be quite threatening.

It will take my job. If an expert does go through the knowledge transfer process, the result will be an expert system that can replace the expert. This is such a threatening possibility for some experts that they are reluctant to participate in the project.

Decimated IS function.   The development of expert systems requires the assignment of computing professionals as knowledge engineers or programmers. Such assignments became problematic in the 1980s due to the impact of cost reduction programs in most firms. Without available people, some firms found that they could not undertake expert system projects.

Need to Kraftize. One answer to the lack of internal resources is to buy an expert system from an outside vendor. This is a viable if the firm agrees to pay the entire development cost of the system. Another approach is to buy an existing expert system, just as most firms buy existing information systems, e.g., Metaphor and Express. One major problem with this approach is the fact that each firm has unique marketing processes and expertise. Discussions with dozens of marketing and information system managers indicates that it is unlikely that one firm will be willing to provide marketing expertise for use by other firms. And, it is equally unlikely that one firm will accept the marketing expertise provided by another firm. A firm such as Kraft tends to believe that they have unique methods and expertise, and want their expert systems to reflect this uniqueness. Thus the need to Kraftize an existing system.

SUCCESS FACTORS

The previous section identified a number of impediments to expert system adoption:

1. Time.
2. Lack of Expertise.
3. " I do not think Jack is better than me."

4. An Expert System is a Model.
5. I rent my knowledge to this firm; why should I put it into an expert system?
6. It will take my job.
7. It will expose what I do, and do not, know.
8. Decimated IS function.
9. Need to Kraftize.

The *Eras of Marketing Systems* paradigm provides a guide to overcoming these impediments because 1) it provides a view of expert systems which is not threatening to marketing managers and 2) focuses on expert systems that can be purchased from outside vendors.

Most marketing managers want to do marketing, not analysis. If expert systems contain marketing knowledge, then marketing managers are threatened. If they analyze data and provide insights based upon this analysis, then the marketing managers view them as assistants, not substitutes. Marketing managers are willing to accept the notion that an analyst is better at analysis than they are, and are thus willing to endorse analytical expertise contained in an expert system. Most managers seem willing to accept the view that moving from the How's business? question to the What's driving the business? question requires the application of models. The importance of obtaining answers to these questions appears to be sufficient to overcome the reluctance to accept models.

The systems reported in this book have characteristics that will prevent their adoption from being overly retarded by the first seven impediments.

The lack of IS professionals can be overcome by out-sourcing – purchasing a system from an outside vendor. This is particularly true when dealing with expert systems that apply analytical knowledge. Most analytical marketing knowledge exists outside the consumer goods firms in universities, consulting firms, and data vendors. It is common for consumer goods firms to go outside for marketing research and modeling projects. It is thus logical for these firms to go outside for systems that apply the knowledge needed for research and modeling projects.

The final impediment, the need to Kraftize a system, can be overcome by the development of a partially filled knowledge base. An outside vendor can identify knowledge that can be applied across firms, and place this knowledge in the knowledge base. This partially filled knowledge base can then be sold to firms on a syndicated basis, along with a consulting service that completes the expert system for each acquiring firm.

AUTHOR INDEX

SUBJECT INDEX